SONGS AND SONNETS ATLANTEAN

Songs and Sonnets Atlantean

by DONALD S. FRYER

ARKHAM HOUSE: Publishers   Sauk City, Wisconsin

1971

CREDITS

Some of the verses in this volume have appeared in the following periodicals:
*The Arkham Collector, Coven 13, Flame Annual, The Galley Sail Review, Haunted,
Macabre, San Francisco, Witchcraft and Sorcery,* and *The Young Physique.*

For permission to quote—in the *Introduction* or the *Notes*—passages from the
following publications: *The Poetical Works of Edmund Spenser,* edited by
J. C. Smith and Ernest de Selincourt, first published and copyright 1912 by
Oxford University Press, London, etc.; *The Prince of Poets, Essays on Edmund
Spenser,* edited by John R. Elliott, Jr., copyright 1968 by New York University;
and *The Renaissance,* by Tucker Brooke and Matthias A. Shaaber, in *A Literary
History of England,* second edition, Volume II, edited by Albert C. Baugh, copy-
right 1967 (original copyright 1948) by Appleton-Century-Crofts;—grateful ac-
knowledgement is made to the following, respectively: Oxford University Press,
Ely House, London; New York University Press, Washington Square, New York;
and Appleton-Century-Crofts, Educational Division of the Meredith Corporation,
New York.

Songs and Sonnets Atlantean

Fragments in Verse and Fragments in Prose

Being translations from the Atlantean,
as well as from the French,
together with a selection of original poems
expressly created by the translator
for the present volume.

Selected and translated
by DONALD S. FRYER

With an Introduction and Notes
by DR. IBID M. ANDOR

Together with commendatory verses
by friends and well-wishers

And featuring numerous dedications
as well as quoted passages.

Acknowledgements

For their warm interest and encouragement, and in some cases over the total period of nine years and seven months, the author is indebted to many persons, especially the following: Dr. Ibid M. Andor, August Derleth, Gloria Kathleen Fryer, George F. Haas, Helen French Hunt, Ian M. Law, Fritz and Jonquil Leiber, Kirby McCauley, Margo Skinner, and Genevieve K. Sully.

And for permission to quote—on the dedication-page—the line "ah but in such an ugly time the true protest is beauty" from the record-album *Pleasures of the Harbor*, words and music by Phil Ochs, issued by A & M Records, Hollywood, California, and copyright 1968 by Barricade Music, Inc.;—grateful acknowledgement is made to Michael Ochs, president of Barricade Music, Inc., Topanga, California. The line in question occurs in the poem by Phil Ochs which appears on the back of the record-jacket and which begins "I've been away for a while but I hope to be back again soon."

DEDICATED,
IN THIS THE REIGN OF ELIZABETH II,
TO THE MEMORY OF EDMUND SPENSER,
POET LAUREATE TO ELIZABETH I.

"ah but in such an ugly time the true protest is beauty"
Phil Ochs, *Pleasures of the Harbor.*

Ah! Colin, whether on the lowly plain,
Piping to shepherds thy sweet roundelays;
Or whether singing in some lofty vein,
Heroic deeds of past or present days;
Or whether in thy lovely mistress's praise,
Thou list to exercise thy learnèd quill;
Thy Muse hath got such grace, and power to please,
With rare invention, beautified by skill,
As who, I pray, therein can ever joy their fill?

O therefore let that happy Muse proceed
To climb the height of Virtue's sacred hill,
Where endless honor shall be made thy meed:

Because no malice of succeeding days
Can rase those records of thy lasting praise.

The *Amoretti and Epithalamion* of Edmund Spenser, first published in 1595:
the second of the two commendatory sonnets by "G. W. Senior, to the Author"—
stanzaically emendated by Donald S. Fryer.

Contents

Introduction

In launching this little argosy of verse upon that vast, darkling, and potentially hostile Ocean Sea known as the general reading public; our poet, Mr. Fryer, offers for the first time in English an extensive selection of poems translated from the Atlantean, even if only through the French of Michel de Labretagne (1493-1550).

The poems have been selected largely from that unique collection by Labretagne, *La Jouvence Bretagnesque,* the original manuscript of which still exists in the Bibliothèque Nationale in Paris. These, the first serious poems by Labretagne after his ingenious but purely apprentice verses done under the tutelage of the Grands Rhétoriqueurs, never saw republication in French until their rediscovery in the nineteenth century by the great critic Sainte-Beuve, who devoted one of the best of his *Causeries du lundi* to Labretagne and his art. Clément Marot (1496-1544), a close personal friend to Labretagne during most of their comparatively short lifetimes, knew and praised the poems highly both before and after their publication. Marot and Labretagne first met in 1519 when Marguerite, later Queen of Navarre, then Duchess of Alençon and Berry, came to visit the Labretagnes at their principal estate located in Brittany, the Château Bretagnesque or Grand Château de Bretagne, bordering on the Gulf of Saint-Malo, not far from the Abbey of Mont-Saint-Michel. Marot belonged at that time to the numerous retinue of Marguerite to whom François I had given him as a page in 1518.

Labretagne, a precocious poet, came of an ancient and noble family who had reigned as *grands seigneurs* in Normandy and Brittany for immemorial centuries and who claimed a direct descent from one of King Arthur's knights. By the time of Marguerite's visit in 1519, Labretagne had already gained an enviable reputation for himself as a distinguished and unique Atlantologist and a student of Atlantean literature, as well as a student of medieval poetry and of Arthurian history as manifested in the Keltic so-called romances of *le roi Artus et ses chevaliers de la Table ronde.* During the years 1517-1519, he circulated his *Jouvence Bretagnesque* in manuscript, becoming widely known as a translator and a lyric poet of considerable distinction, even if of limited output. Marot and Labretagne became instant and life-long friends after a comparison of poetic notes, and Marot urged Labretagne to publish sans further delay his collection, which accordantly appeared in 1520. Labretagne in his turn encouraged Marot, and contributed financially to the publication, in 1532, of Marot's own first collection *L'Adolescence Clémentine,* besides affording him a place of refuge on divers occasions when Marot was in disfavor with the King. But it was not until after his death that Labretagne achieved his greatest fame, and this as a novelist. His later poems, all original pieces, did not see publication until their inclusion, under the title *Dernier testament poétique,* in the *Oeuvres complètes* published in 1633.

Many of the early translations by Labretagne, sometimes considerably recast, reappeared in the author's famous romance, *Le roman de la princesse Aïs et du prince Atlantaryon,* published posthumously 1550-1555 in Lyons, and issued in ninety volumes, the longest novel in any language, with the total pagination running over 30,000. All of these poems from the Atlantean (including those in this book) do not survive except in the French translations of Labretagne; unless the originals may be contained and yet identified on the recently-discovered volumes, or scrolls, from the submerged libraries of Atlantis and Poseidonis. In making his translations through the French, Mr. Fryer has followed the text of the poems in their first appearance in *La Jouvence Bretagnesque,* preferring the simpler early versions to the elaborate, even if more polished, later ones.

Before we pass to a discussion of Atlantean poetry and its principal forms, as well as of how some of it happened to survive, we should consider, however briefly, the one and only collection of poetry published by Labretagne during his lifetime and the place it holds in the history of French literature. Although a former pupil of the Grands Rhétoriqueurs, little of the poetical tricks of the latter appear in this his first serious poetry. While some of his work in verse has a certain affinity with that of Marot (who had also been a pupil of the Grands Rhétoriqueurs), Labretagne anticipates the renaissance of French poetry

brought about by the poets of the Pléiade, besides anticipating the work
of Agrippa d'Aubigné. About one-third of the *Jouvence* are original
poems influenced by medieval and Atlantean lyric poetry; the rest are
translations of Atlantean odes, songs, "sonnets" (id est, songs archroyal), etc., taken from the night-fabled *Codex Atlanteanus*. However,
virtually all of the translations from the Atlantean are paraphrases in
French prose, a sort of vers libre not unlike the verses in the King James
Bible, nor unlike the *petits poèmes en prose* of Aloÿsius Bertrand
(1807-1841) in his *Gaspard de la Nuit* (1842). Labretagne and Marot,
it will be noted, were among the first to cultivate the sonnet in French,
and to do so with distinction. There can be little doubt but that *La
Jouvence Bretagnesque* afforded a major impetus to the poets of the
Pléiade, in showing them the possibilities of French in creating a poetry
comparable to the best of the ancient Greeks and Latins, or of the ancient Atlanteans.

It is one of the greatest literary ironies of all time that the *Codex
Atlanteanus,* that unique collection of Atlantean manuscripts, should
have survived some 15,000 years, only to meet utter destruction during
the French Revolution in the sacking and razing of the Château
Bretagnesque. The history of the *Codex Atlanteanus* is so well known
as scarcely to bear repetition; but perhaps the patient reader will bear
with the present Atlantologist while he refreshes the reader's memory
with a brief summary.

After the foundering of one-half or one-third of Atlantis the Archkingdom and virtually all of the Empire of Atlantis through the action
of the Great Cataclysm about 13,000 B.C., the Atlantean garrisons
were retained in the forts and watchtowers in what are now Cornwall,
Wales, and southern Ireland. Aänsess, and Archknight, and the governor
of the Atlantean holdings in these lands, was made a Grand Archknight
by the King sometime shortly after the Great Cataclysm. After their
thirtieth wedding anniversary, Atlantarion and Aïs, then King and
Queen of the much-diminished Atlantean Empire, repeated the itinerary
of their original wedding voyage (although taking much less time to do
it the second time than the first), visiting the sites of the former island

kingdoms—a rather gray and funereal trip save for their sojourn in Wales at Apenderragon the Great Watchtower in southern Valoth, or Wales, as guests of Aänsess. The King and Aänsess, both of them poets, had been close friends and correspondents, despite a considerable difference in age, ever since they had first met sometime before the Great Cataclysm. During this last visit with Aänsess in Valoth, the King made him a Grand Archknight Prince.

After the second wedding voyage of Aïs and Atlantarion, the governor and the King continued their correspondence, as well as their exchange of notes poetic and otherwise; and some thirteen years later, the garrisons were no longer considered necessary and were recalled by the King. The Grand Archknight Prince sealed his records, correspondence, and manuscripts with those of the preceding governors in the lowermost vaults of the central tower of Apenderragon (these were duplicates only—the originals had always been sent to Atlantis), and closed for the last time all the outer gates leading to the Great Watchtower. Thus, the Atlanteans abandoned their holdings in what are now the British Isles, leaving those lands forever. Escorted by a military flotilla, Aänsess returned in his own private trireme to Atlantis the Archkingdom. After a lengthy visit with the King at the Outhanox, the Great Citadel of Poseidonis (in Xonorr, the capital of that great mountain-heart-land), he retired to his place of birth, his family's ancestral estate located in the great pastureland of the Astazhan, which occupied all of southeastern Atlantis. Upon his death, the King erected—within the castle-gardens of the old estate—an elaborate and beautiful monument to house his remains.

Centuries passed, and the duplicate scrolls of Aänsess, together with those of his predecessors, lay undisturbed in the lowermost vaults of the old central mass of the Great Watchtower whose upper and middle sections fell away into ruin, leaving only the massive foundations intact. Later, after many successive invasions by outlanders, a Saxon lord incorporated the ruined watchtower into the donjon of his castle. During the reign of Uther Pendragon, the resident family of nobles discovered the *Codex Atlanteanus,* as it became called. Later still, it was brought to King Arthur's court at Camelot, and became part of the Royal Library there. Through the supreme intelligence as well as the arts magical of

Merlin, both a great scholar and an archimage, the clerk-scholars at Arthur's court deciphered the *Codex* and translated it into Latin and Welch. As pieced together by Merlin and as narrated by the troubadours and minstrels instructed by him, the story of the vanished world of Atlantis, and the last days of its Empire, created a great sensation at court, particularly the romance of the Princess Aïs and the Prince Atlantarion.

Long after Camelot had fallen into ruin, the *Codex Atlanteanus,* as well as the Latin and Welch translations, somehow still extant in a now-buried vault of the old Royal Library, were discovered in the thirteenth century and given as gifts by the then King of England to the Abbey of Mont-Saint-Michel, to form part of the library there. During the fourteenth century, the *Codex* and the translations of the same were acquired by the Labretagnes and became part of their library kept in an old tower called "la Tour d'yvoire"—there the young Michel de Labretagne discovered them in 1503, and with the aid of the earlier Authurian translations, rendered the *Codex* into French. Much of the material he used in his famous *Roman,* incorporating some of it bodily into the novel. After an elaborate and painstaking preparation, Labretagne began the actual writing of his novel about 1529 and continued working on it until his death in 1550.

Although *Le roman de la princesse Aïs et du prince Atlantaryon* ranks as one of the first great novels of modern European literature, and although its publication in 1550-1555 marks one of the high watermarks of French Renaissance printing, strangely enough no one thought of issuing in published form the actual *Codex* itself, or any of the translations of the same. Thus, together with many beautiful and valuable medieval illuminated manuscripts, the *Codex Atlanteanus,* as well as the Arthurian and French translations, survived until 1791 when the entire library containing these and other materials was destroyed utterly during the French Revolution in the general plundering and burning of the Château Bretagnesque.

Virtually all of our present information about Atlantis and Atlantean poetry derives either from the *Roman* of Labretagne, or from such of his notes as are preserved with *La Jouvence Bretagnesque* in the Bibliothèque Nationale in Paris. The principal forms of Atlantean poetry, according to Labretagne, are as follows: the song or little song, usually one to nine lines but never more than nine; the song or great song, or epic poem, generally employing all known forms, and of variable length; the sonnet or song archroyal, usually ten to twenty lines, rarely more; the ode or apostrophe, of any length but usually more than thirty lines; and finally a form very much like the French poem in prose as invented and elaborated by Aloÿsius Bertrand and Charles Pierre Baudelaire (poems of this nature were always written in a rich purple ink wherefrom derived the Atlantean names of the "purple patch" or "purple poem" or "purple prose"). The great song or epic poem was invariably used for detailed narratives whether long or short. The Atlanteans had a predilection for long, rather Whitmanesque, lines. True rime was not employed but something very much like assonance-rime was used, especially in poems of more than one stanza wherein the stanzas would be interlinked by rime. This use, in Atlantean poetry, of a system of interlinking rimes, whether assonance or otherwise, is somewhat analogous in English to the system of interlinking rimes employed by Edmund Spenser in the stanza that bears his name or by Spenser and Alexander Montgomery in their identically similar sonnet-form, evidently evolved independently of each other.

Unlike Labretagne who translated the Atlantean originals into French prose and who evidently despaired of achieving with true rime an effect in French similar to that achieved by assonance-rime in Atlantean; Mr. Fryer—undeterred by the originals in Atlantean because of their express absence—has courageously elected to achieve, with true rime, translations into English verse that would approximate the original effect in Atlantean. It may be argued that the results are not real translations but recreations into another language, and through the possibly obfuscatory medium of yet another language at that. This may be true but we must grant Mr. Fryer the right of his carefully considered choice, whether the poems assembled in the present volume fail or succeed simply as translations, or recreations, and/or as original creations. As the most logical equivalent in English into which to translate the Atlantean "little song," he has chosen to Spenserian stanza. For the Atlantean "sonnet" or song archroyal, there is no true equivalent readily at hand. According to Labretagne, "this prince of fixed forms in Atlantean poetry" has three sections, with each one successively shorter than the preceding (although the lines of each succeeding section usually are progressively longer), and with each section linked to the preceding one by a system of assonance-rimes. To do justice to this unique tripartite form in Atlantean prosody as described by Labretagne and as manifested by him in his paraphrases in French prose, it has proven mandatory for Mr. Fryer to innovate a special form of the Spenserian sonnet, consisting of a Spenserian stanza, a tercet, and a couplet. This innovation he terms, accordantly, the Spenserian stanza-sonnet.

The original Spenserian sonnet itself, unlike the Spenserian stanza, is a form that has found virtually no, or very little, employment in English since its use by Edmund Spenser, Alexander Montgomery, and a few other poets of their time. Devoting itself exclusively to the publication of sonnets, as its title indicates; the poetry magazine *The Sonnet, Dedicated to the Memory of Sir Thomas Wyatt and of Henry Howard Earl of Surrey,* and published in the first quarter of the present century, does not contain one single Spenserian sonnet in any issue of its complete run. The Spenserian stanza itself, in terms of its actual use by poets, has declined steadily since around 1900, and finds virtually no employment at all today, oddly enough, in this the Neo-Elizabethan Age.

The Spenserian stanza, it will be recalled, consists of two quatrains and a final alexandrine (or, very rarely, a fourteener), all of which are linked by rime: A B A B / B C B C / C. The Spenserian sonnet consists of three quatrains and a final couplet, with the quatrains linked by rime: A B A B / B C B C / C D C D / E E. The reader will note that the rime-scheme of the Spenserian stanza as well as that of the first nine lines of the Spenserian sonnet are thus exactly the same. The Spenserian stanza-sonnet wherein unite the stately Spenserian stanza and the even more stately Spenserian sonnet, consists of a Spenserian stanza, a tercet, and a couplet, with the Spenserian stanza and the tercet linked by rime, as follows: A B A B B C B C C / D C D / E E. Usually alexandrines or fourteeners, the tercet and the couplet are thus linked in terms of length of line. This further development will prove that the Spenserian sonnet—by shewing forth the Spenserian stanza "hidden" within it, and by arranging the tercet and the couplet as lines longer than the usual pentameter—is as stately as, or is more stately than (due to its greater length), the Spenserian stanza, and is accordantly the stateliest of all sonnet-forms in English or, possibly, in any language.

Another feature of the Spenserian stanza-sonnet which the reader will note in some of the poems assembled herein, is the rondeau-like device whereby line three more or less repeats as line thirteen (the first line of the final couplet), and line one more or less repeats as line fourteen (the second line of the final couplet); both lines usually lengthened, and hence both with appropriate additions and/or alterations. Through this device, amongst others, Mr. Fryer hopes to restore to the sonnet or *sonetto*—that is, "little song" (in Italian)—some of its original, purely *singing,* qualities.

Needless to add, in view of the subject-matter and the consequent style of the poems originally in Atlantean and/or in French, as well as in view of the subject-matter of the original poems expressly created by the translator for the present volume, it has proven essential that Mr. Fryer utilize (in his English) that which for lack of better terms we must call "the grand manner" and "the solemn tone"—in short, the incantatory mode—thereby restoring to poetic diction certain words or phrases ordinarily considered today as being outmoded, at least by the poetic fashions of the moment. These words and phrases our poet has found it highly necessary to use in view of certain subtle considerations of style, tone, meaning, and emphasis, as well as in view of certain similarly subtle effects which may be achieved thereby, effects impossible to achieve in any other way.

Thus, this volume has two principal purposes: to render into English the first considerable body of poems from the Atlantean, and to render direct homage to the *poet* (1552?-1599), and not the dramatist, whom the Elizabethans themselves held as supreme. That the poetry of Edmund Spenser should find comparatively little appreciation and admiration in our century, is of no great consequence; the reasons for this temporary neglect are perfectly apparent to the perceptive lover and student of literature; Spenser's time will come again as it did in Elizabethan times or in the time of the English Romantic poets, as well as in the time of their subsequent public vogue. But that the unique, merely historical, importance of Spenser's poetry should be obscured as a result of this curious neglect, is nothing less than a stain on the vast escutcheon of literature in English. If in 1912 Ernest de Selincourt could make the observation "that of late years the poetry of Spenser has occupied far less attention than is warranted either by its own intrinsic beauty or by its importance as a vital influence upon the development of our literature"—then we can make, alas! the same observation today with even greater truth.

Yet this is the man and poet of whom the same Ernest de Selincourt has written, and justly, in his magnificent *Introduction* to the Oxford Spenser: ". . . The true memorial to Spenser is to be read in the work of his successors. He is among the very greatest of our poets, but the significance of his poetry in the history of our literature is even greater than its intrinsic value. He recreated English prosody, giving back to our verse the fluidity and the grace that it had lost since the days of Chaucer, and extending the range of its achievement; he created English poetic diction, lifting it from anarchy and stiffness, daring greatly, but triumphing whether in the simple or the ornate, widening its scope, but at the same time never failing to give it ease and flexibility, so that language became to him a willing servant, and could voice the subtlest shades of mood or fancy. By means of this rich and varied style, fully expressive of his high seriousness, his spirituality, his inexhaustible sense of beauty, he has exercised a spell that has been potent for three centuries, and none has called so many poets to their vocation."

True, there has appeared in these the 1960's just past a goodly number of outstanding books on Spenser, each of them shedding a greater light on usually one or more facets of his extra-ordinary creative genius, and some of them emphasizing his unique formal as well as thematic originality. Some of these books must needs be mentioned here.

Short Time's Endless Monument, The symobolism of the numbers in Edmund Spenser's "Epithalamion," by A. Kent Hieatt (Columbia University Press, New York, 1960), brilliantly elucidates the ingenious numerological symbolism that forms the organic core of Spenser's own marriage ode.

A Preface to "The Faerie Queene," by Graham Hough (W. W. Norton and Company, Inc., New York, 1962), ably summarizes the sources and authors (the Carolingian and Arthurian mytho-poetic cycles, Boiardo, Ariosto, Tasso, etc.) directly or indirectly influencing Spenser, and makes a simple and brief but good beginning use of Freud's *Interpretation of Dreams* in an attempt at understanding the structure of *The Faerie Queene,* which thus becomes a dream-poem (with concomitant dream-symbolism) possessing (as John Symonds urges for Ariosto's epic *Orlando Furioso*) "the unity of a vast piece of tapestry rather than of archietecture."

The Poetry of Edmund Spenser, A Study, by William Nelson (Columbia University Press, New York and London, 1963), contends that all of Spenser's poetry, but especially *The Faerie Queene,* is carefully structured around and out from an intellectual core or centre; and that theme, rather than story, is the chief governing principle: over-all, this book is a carefully balanced and highly competent appraisal of the entire *corpus* of Spenser's poetry.

Spenser and the Numbers of Time, by Alastair Fowler (Barnes and Noble, Inc., New York, 1964), employing the *modus operandi* of *Short Time's Endless Monument,* ingeniously and brilliantly demonstrates how divers numerological systems (classical and medieval, popular and arcane) operate organically to create the unique structure of *The Faerie Queene.* In the words of the publisher: "Regarded in this way, the poem emerges as a cosmic model constructed in 'narrow verse' with masterful economy and subtlety."

The Kindly Flame, A Study of the Third and Fourth Books of "The Faerie Queene," by Thomas P. Roche, Jr. (Princeton University Press, Princeton, New Jersey, 1964), seeks to show, in an admirably clear and sensitive way, that Spenser was just as much in control of the structure of Books III and IV as he was in control of that of Books I and II; that the lengends of chastity and friendship demand their complex and interwoven system of narratives to exemplify Spenser's or any other truly realistic conception of the virtues in question.

Spenser's Image of Nature, Wild Man and Shepherd in "The Faerie Queene," by Donald Cheney (Yale University Press, New Haven and London, 1966), in demonstrating that pastoral elements counterpoint the epic motifs throughout *The Faerie Queene,* attempts to follow the poem's overt sequence of presentation rather than forcing upon it a foreign conceptual framework, and argues for a parallelism of structure in Books V and VI similar to the same in Books I and II: paramount in this study is the author's "close attention to continually shifting ironic perspectives."

Spenser's World of Glass, A Reading of "The Faerie Queene," by Kathleen Williams (University of California Press, Berkeley and Los Angeles, 1966), reveals with an admirable freshness, grace, and lucidity that *The Faerie Queene* depends for its unity upon a pattern of meaning established and expanded throughout the six books but coherent and self-consistent at the end of each; this particular study seems to sum up the new spirit in Spenserian criticism probably better than any other book mentioned here.

The Poetry of "The Faerie Queene," by Paul J. Alpers (Princeton University Press, Princeton, New Jersey, 1967), while indicating a variety of approaches to *The Faerie Queene,* urges readers and students alike to return to the surface metaphor (with emphasis on line and stanza rather than canto and book) for the poem's meaning rather than seeking that meaning in rigid and arid theories or conceptual frameworks; the author takes to task many of the oher notable Spenserians of our time for approaching Spenser in a way either over-elaborate or inadequately simple.

Spenser's Images of Life, by C. S. Lewis, edited by Alastair Fowler (Cambridge University Press, London and New York, 1967), contends that much in Spenser must be seen as "pageant," that Spenser's pageantries must be experienced with some knowledge of Neo-Platonism and of Renaissance iconography (including pageant proper, tournament pageantry, masque, traditional images of gods, hieroglyphs and emblems, and philosophical iconography), and that *The Faerie Queene* is not an epic but rather is a grand pageant of the cosmos or of Nature and thus is Spenser's Hymn to Life: a worthy companion-piece to Lewis's earlier and largely Spenserian study *The Allegory of Love* (The Clarendon Press, Oxford, 1936), even though Lewis himself did not live to write this book as extant in its published form.

Flower on a Lowly Stalk, The Sixth Book of the Faerie Queene, by Arnold Williams (Michigan State University Press, East Lansing, 1967), gives a sensitive and perceptive reading of Book VI in the first book-length study devoted to the same, and presents a thorough, sound, lucid, and gracious analysis of Spenser's narrative, the meaning of that narrative, plus all the effects of "affect," with an especially welcome emphasis on Spenser's usually-overlooked gift for comedy, as well as his gift for overt oral verse techniques.

Spenser's Allegory of Justice in the Fifth Book of the Faerie Queene, by T. K. Dunseath (Princeton University Press, Princeton, New Jersey, 1968), gives a thoughtful and long-overdue defense of the least-liked, most-neglected, and most-misunderstood book of *The Faerie Queene* in the first book-length study devoted to the same, and shows that Spenser, in giving us a highly repressive picture of justice in a fallen world, was just as much in command of his fictional art in Book V as anywhere else in *The Faerie Queene.*

Reading Spenser, An Introduction to "The Faerie Queene," by Roger Sale (Random House, New York, 1968), emphasizes Spenser's sense of life rather than attempting to deal with his encyclopedic range of ideas and symbologies, and is remarkable for manifesting just how much even a person insensitive to his style can derive from *The Faerie Queene,* even if he deliberately underestimates or makes little of Books, IV, V, and VI, as well as the Mutabilitie Cantoes.

Some of the same writers whose books have been cited above contribute salient essays to the following three volumes which present much valuable supplementary material toward understanding Spenser's thought and style.

Elizabethan Poetry, Modern Essays in Criticism, edited by Paul J. Alpers (Oxford University Press, New York and London, 1967), containing much solid scholarship, devotes considerable attention to Spenser, with the last one-third of the book given over to *The Faerie Queene,* and helps provide a convenient index to the major re-evaluation of Spenser, and his *oeuvre,* that has come about in the 1960's.

Spenser, A Collection of Critical Essays, edited by Harry Berger, Jr. (Prentice-Hall, Englewood Cliffs, New Jersey, 1968), draws upon the ideas and literary techniques of all ages to provide a wide spectrum of thought and opinion on divers themes, metaphors, and problems inherent in Spenser's over-all *oeuvre,* from his earliest published work to his last.

The Prince of Poets, Essays on Edmund Spenser, edited by John R. Elliott, Jr. (New York University Press, New York and University of London Press, London, 1968), presents both a valuable documentary survey of Spenser's varying poetic reputation through more than three and a half centuries, as well as an introduction to the chief problems posed by his poetry to the modern reader, with especial emphasis on the poetic values of his own age.

It is highly significant that the editor of the last-cited volume not only employs the title that he does but moreover states in his *Introduction:* "Perhaps no major English poet has received a more appreciative re-reading in recent times than Edmund Spenser. For years relegated to the dusty shelf reserved for authors politely honored but seldom read, Spenser has been one of the chief beneficiaries of our renewed interest in and understanding of Renaissance art. With the discovery by modern readers of the intellectual complexity and artistic coherence of literary forms that once seemed merely naive and disordered, Spenser has emerged from the shadow of Marlowe, Shakespeare, and Donne to lay claim once again to his title as 'the Prince of Poets in his tyme' [in the words of the inscription on the monument to Spenser in Westminster Abbey]."

Although Spenser—of all the great elder poets in English—has probably received the least circulation, the least understanding, and the least appreciation in the twentieth century until recently, yet it is heartening to observe how diverse have been the admirers of "the Prince of Poets" in our own time; these have included not only such recognized Spenserians like the great C. S. Lewis himself but—just as important—such unlikely figures (unlikely at least at first glance) as Virginia Wolff, T. S. Eliot, F. Scott Fitzgerald, and Louis MacNeice. But however heartening such an observation might prove, and however heartening the recent wealth of unusually intelligent and well-informed books on Spenser, yet we must repeat here the statement made in 1912 by Ernest de Selincourt, speaking apropos of Spenser, that "A full interpretation of his genius, worthy of its theme, is yet to be written." Such an interpretation would amalgamate the best and most generous approaches to Spenser whether made long ago or whether made in the present, especially those included in the outstanding studies on Spenser published in these the 1960's just past. And such an interpretation would resolve as far as possible the problem of the over-all pattern structuring *The Faerie Queene,* and would syncretize the better solutions to this problem that recent scholars have proffered.

It may appear that we are laying an undue emphasis on the form, that is, the structure, and (evolving from the structure) the movement of *The Faerie Queene.* But it is only through an apprehension of its formal pattern (as the same circles or cycles through time and space) that we may gain any real understanding of this great poem's ultimate over-all meaning. Actually the truth of the structure of *The Faerie Queene,* as well as of its meaning, lies undoubtedly somewhere between Graham Hough's dream-poem with concomitant dream-symbolism, Alastair Fowler's numerological symbolism, and William Nelson's intellectual and thematic solution. Of course, in the most profound sense, this greatest poem by Spenser, with its ever-changing imagery, is a fantasy, a conscious dream, supremely a work of the imagination. This fact is in itself one of the first keys to understanding the poem and its peculiar construction.

Indeed, although the fact is often overlooked, *The Faerie Queene* is not only the first great fantasy in modern English, having crystallized many of what are now familiar conceptions of *faërie* and of the light fantastical, but it includes moreover—amidst its vast spectrum of tone and subject—the first delineation of the weird and the darkly fantastic as we understand them today. This is pointed out inferentially by the late great H. P. Lovecraft, that "literary Copernicus" (to use Fritz Leiber's memorable term), in his classic study *Supernatural Horror in Literature*: ". . . By the time the old Northern myths take literary form, and in that later time when the weird appears as a steady element in the literature of the day, we find it mostly in metrical dress; as indeed we find the greater part of the strictly imaginative writing of the Middle Ages and Renaissance. The Scandinavian Eddas and Sagas thunder with cosmic horror, and shake with the stark fear of Ymir and his shapeless spawn; whilst our own Anglo-Saxon Beowulf and the later Continental Nibelung tales are full of eldritch weirdness. Dante is a pioneer in the classic capture of macabre atmosphere, and in Spenser's stately stanzas will be seen more than a few touches of fantastic terror in landscape, incident, and character." Indeed, properly defined, *The Faerie Queene* not only presents the first conscious "olden" style in modern English— or for that matter the first conscious style, or rather spectrum of styles, as we comprehend such today,—but it also represents the first "Romanticism" (as understood in the sense of the Arthurian and Carolingian romances) as well as the first great "Gothic" fiction in modern English, in the most inclusive definition of those expressions.

To an earlier commentator, the French authority on English literature Émile Legouis (1861-1937), *The Faerie Queene* appears primarily as a dreamlike pageant of constantly evolving and dissolving imagery the which, as presented through the recurring music of the Spenserian stanza, lulls the reader's intellectual faculties asleep. Legouis' book *Spenser* (E. P. Dutton, New York and J. M. Dent, London and Toronto, 1926) reduces itself in essence to a consideration of Spenser's poetry, and *The Faerie Queene* above all, as a tastefully assembled collection of imagery. Essentially it is a restatement of the stance of William Hazlitt and Leigh Hunt, or of the English Romantic poets, who certainly understood the poem in small parts and parcels but not in the mass, although undoubtedly they may have instinctively felt or sensed the over-all structure. (Coleridge comes the closest to a true comprehension and appreciation.) Legouis himself perceives nothing of the true structural principles animating *The Faerie Queene,* even though, unbeknownst to himself, he clearly held the first key to understanding the mystery. He does do justice to Spenser's overt, that is, surface, artistry. He does recognize "his inexhaustible sense of beauty" but of "his high seriousness," of "his spirituality," and of his over-all moral or ethical purpose (that is, in Spenser's case, his over-all *artistic* purpose), Legouis deliberately makes little. Typically, he is completely insensitive to the cosmic element in Spenser. To Legouis, Spenser is above all else a creator of imagery, and really little beyond this. But even this does not really minimize Spenser. To some critics and poetic mentors (e.g., Ambrose Bierce), imagery is the heart, the soul, the essense of poetry: it *is* the poetry. Even by such a restrictive definition as this one, Spenser still emerges as the most poetic of poets.

Whether one agrees or disagrees with their divers theses, such books as these are surely welcome, such books as these are surely needed. They widen our understanding of Spenser, or they stimulate us into providing our own solutions to certain mysteries inherent in his greatest work, and they enhance our appreciation of his unique genius. But they do so under a scholarly aegis rather than purely a poetical one. This is not a criticism, it is merely an observation. Today Spenser may be "the scholar's poet" but tomorrow he may yet again be "the poet's poet" as he was yesterday to the Elizabethans and to the English Romantic poets.

Whether or not Spenser could ever again become "the people's poet" remains to be seen. For, in spite of the fact that Spenser was the supreme literary celebrity of his own age; in spite of the fact that *The Faerie Queene* was to the Elizabethans themselves their supreme work of art; in spite of the fact that his poetry proved a great and beneficent influence—a source of delight, vision, wisdom, and technical instruction —to virtually all the other great English poets coming after him (beginning with Kit Marlowe and Will Shakespeare and continuing on through the English Romantic and Victorian poets); in spite of the fact that this same poetry, whether directly or indirectly, has continued to be a great and beneficent influence on virtually all of literature in modern English even into our own century; in spite of the fact that the recent wealth of unusually intelligent and well-informed studies on Spenser and *The Faerie Queene* have succeeded in rehabilitating his critical reputation; and in spite of the fact that Spenser is in essence the very father —the very fountainhead as it were—of literature, poetry, and fantasy in modern English;—it cannot be denied that for the average reader Spenser's great fairy tale has become the lost Atlantis of our older literature, the great "lost" classic of early modern English. For since around 1900, more or less coinciding with the death of Queen Victoria and with the inevitable decline of the British Empire, *The Faerie Queene* has fallen from the common currency that it once enjoyed in the homes of English-speaking families all over the world. For at one time Spenser's great myth—uniquely fusing as it does classical epic, medieval romance, and medieval allegory—was one of the great family classics, together with the King James Bible and the complete works of Shakespeare. If this great work—once universally accepted as the great *English* epic— does gain common currency again, it will not be primarily through the medium of the printed page but in some dramatic and novel fashion hitherto unsuspected. If this book of "songs and sonnets Atlantean" however modestly helps in any way to restore Shakespeare's own master to common currency—whether amongst the poets or, more importantly, amongst the people—then its publication will be more than justified.

Thus, whether Neo-Elizabethan, Neo-Spenserian, Neo-Baroque, or Baroque Late Romantic—whatever designation seems most appropriate —the present volume is a deliberate postscript to that specific tradition of "pure poetry" begun in modern English by Edmund Spenser and more or less ended by such Californian lyric poets as George Sterling (1869-1926), Nora May French (1881-1907), and Clark Ashton Smith (1893-1961). If nothing else (and this alone might prove enough), this little volume bears witness to the fact that there are still more than a few brave souls who can see beyond the desolation of T. S. Eliot's *Waste Land* to the manifold and labyrinthine greenery of Spenser's Faeryland, to the allegorical dream-garden that flourishes in *Le Roman de la Rose,* to the primordial splendors of the archetypal Eden.

It is then altogether appropriate that this volume—dedicated as it is to the memory of the supreme poet of the Age of Elizabeth I (1558-1603)—should appear as of the nonce in this the Age of Elizabeth II (begun 1952). Thus, insofar as it brings together for the first time in English an extensive selection of poems translated from the Atlantean; and insofar as it brings to the attention of poets a new form well worthy of their use, to wit, the Spenserian stanza-sonnet; and insofar as it recalls attention, in however an humble manner, to one of the greatest of poets in English or any language, under a poetical rather than a scholarly aegis (and insofar as it attempts to recall attention, even if only incidentally, to one of the most magnificent forms in English prosody, to wit, the Spenserian stanza);—this major contribution to Plato's Atlantis Mythos (within the minor compass of "narrow verse") may be modestly recommended.

—Dr. Ibid M. Andor

Atlantis Hall, Terceira, the Azores.
30 September 1970.

> If music and sweet poetry agree,
> As they must needs, the sister and the brother,
> Then must the love be great twixt thee and me,
> Because thou lovest the one, and I the other.
> Dowland to thee is dear, whose heavenly touch
> Upon the lute doth ravish human sense;
> Spenser to me, whose deep conceit is such
> As passing all conceit, needs no defense.
> Thou lovest to hear the sweet melodious sound
> That Phoebus's lute, the queen of music, makes;
> And I in deep delight am chiefly drowned
> Whenas himself to singing he betakes.
> One god is god of both, as poets feign;
> One knight loves both, and both in thee remain.

Shakespeare, *The Passionate Pilgrim.*

SONGS AND SONNETS ATLANTEAN

AVALONESSYS

Translated from the French of Michel de Labretagne.

When Avalon and Lyonnesse and Yss were one
Above the Ocean Sea's eternal hiss and spray;
When west of Wales and Cornwall, Avalonessys lay,—
A sea-green pearl in a shoaling sea; where the sun,
With thread of orichalch, its time-web splendent spun;
Where knight and lady Atlantean, midst fountains' play,
Upon the sea-green sod would wend their whilesome way,
Whenas the world waxed old, with Time long since begun. . . .

It was then, it was there that I loved you, my love,
With paradisiacal flames as ragingly afire
As any star within the empery of night;

Until that final day when ocean's wine, above,
Did loom afoam and, down, did fall—one wave entire—
To drown the fires of love, of life, and all of light.

THE CROWN AND TRIDENT IMPERIAL

Translated from the Atlantean of an unknown poet.

1. Let us muse upon the more than splendor, upon the wonder and the marvel, that Atlantis was of old, and above all else, let us muse upon the crown and trident, and its ensamples manifold: Let us consider first the wide brow-encircling band from whose upper rim rise the nine tall, three-sided, and outward-pointing spikes . . . then, within and overtopping a little the encircling spikes, the conical cap . . . then, rising from the top of the cap, the smaller quasi-diamond-shape . . . then, rising from the diamond-shape, the short shaft that supports an imperial, rectilinear, and sharp-headed trident, of which the middle tooth overtops a little the two attendant teeth. Thus, the archetype, and innumerable the variants thereof devised by the artists and artisans of Atlantis, in substances multifarious, even in that rarest metal of all . . . the curious and costly alloy which immingles copper and gold with some silver . . . the pale flame-gold of orichalch. . . .

2. Of the crown and trident, once upon a time you could have found ensamples everywhere. . . . Useless abstraction to repeat them here, for the world in which they were once more than manifest has disappeared. Only in silhouette upon small coins preserved from the elder time can you still find this heraldry . . . or only fixed upon the top of single columns that still rise up in the wilderness, or by the lonely sea, or high in the desolate mountains. . . .

3. And shall anyone forge anew, and once more from orichalchum, the most sacred ensample of all? . . . the sceptre-staff now lost but once belonging to the Archking of the Empire of Atlantis . . . the thrice-tripled trident above the single crown. . . .

ATLANTIS

Translated from the Atlantean of Athallarion.

An alpha huge athwart the Ocean Sea,
The island continent Atlantis, old
In thrice-resplendent sovereign empery,
Uprose from deeps now deeper still. In gold
And orichalch it pleased her to enfold
The pomp, the pride, of her imperial court;
Where Beauty flamed her flambeaux manifold,
And blazing Wealth maintained its foremost port,
Enshrined—O Empire's heart—in Empire's uttermost fort:—

O fortress . . . pharos . . . archsublime acropolis of kings;
Where once the crown and trident swayed that pompous prideful court
Where Majesty in splendent state would muse on splendid things. . . .

O Splendor sunk, alas! beyond recall, that once of yore
Her crown and trident's empire stretched from east to western shore. . . .

Alas! And now no more . . . For ever more. . . . Alas!

THE ROSE AND THE THORN

Translated from the French of Michel de Labretagne.

This red red rose, first rooted and tended tenderly
     in the red of my heart,
And then to the garden of our love transplanted
     with tender trembling art,
This red red rose, this life's love's heart's blood's
     bloom, this do you scorn,
Caressing instead, you sweet perversity shaped like a
     lass, its well-pricked guardians of thorn.

ROSE ESCARLATE

Translated from the French of Michel de Labretagne.

In the garden of our love have we grown a scarlet rose
That flames it fiercely to the sun and gleams it to the moon;
But when our love falls to decay, and passion in silence goes,
Then the scarlet rose turns pale, lost in a deathly swoon.

"O EBON-COLORED ROSE"

Translated from the Atlantean of Prince Atlantarion.

> "Ces fleurs maladives."
> Baudelaire, *Les Fleurs du Mal,* dedication.

> ". . . Ebon blooms that swell in ghastly woods . . ."
> Robert E. Howard, *Which Will Scarcely Be Understood.*

> "Not such as earth out of her fruitful womb
> Throws forth to men, sweet and well-savorèd,
> But direful deadly black, both leaf and bloom,
> Fit to adorn the dead, and deck the dreary tomb."
> Edmund Spenser, *The Faerie Queene,* II: VII: LI.

The rose blooms ebon in these longsome latter years,
These long, too long, autumnal afternoons and nights.
Her darkling petals sparkle not with dew but tears. . . .
The dearling dew of lovers' dusk no more delights
Her languid leaves, nor traces errant loving flights
Upon her face, but in that same dew's sparkling stead
Burn bitter salty tears with pallid paling lights,
The paling mournful lamps of dying loves and dead,
Whose flames with oils of grief, and shame,
    and wan distress, are fed. . . .

Like night-black vipers that we overlate beware,
The darkling thorns lurk low, close to the rose's bed,
And sullenly distill the venom called Despair. . . .

And when the mournful lamps shall dim,
    shall fail, shall utterly leave no light,
Then shall the ebon rose be lost,
    lost in the cosmic waste of Night.

YOUR MOUTH OF POMEGRANATE

Translated from the Atlantean of Prince Atlantarion.

Your mouth of pomegranate mixed with musk is mine:
When I, and I alone, unseal your bright-red lips,
The bright-red pomegranate-blossom of your lips,
Your breath divine with musk breathes forth to me, and then
I breathe a fragrance as of pomegranate-wine,
A rich, rubescent wine long-stored in darkling vaults....
And then, within the garnet cup that is your mouth,
I taste a savor subtly tart and subtly sweet,
The distillation of the pomegranate-fruit,
Such as might grow within a garden-close of gods....

And thus, beneath the branches of these trees in bloom,
These Atlantean pomegranate-trees abloom
With the bright-red waxy stars of pomegranate-flowers,
When sinks and sets the pomegranate-colored sun
Beyond the wine of pomegranate-colored seas,
Then do I press my mouth on your mouth: O my love,
Your mouth of pomegranate mixed with musk is mine!

AS BUDS AND BLOSSOMS IN THE
MONTH OF MAY THE ROSE

Translated from the French of Pierre de Ronsard.

As buds and blossoms in the month of May the rose,
In all the youth and beauty of her firstling bloom;
With such a jealous flush the eastern skies illume
When tears of dew the dawn upon her face bestows;

Deep in her heart, empetalled Love and Grace repose,
Making the groves and gardens redolent with perfume;
But, when too harsh a rain or sun entrains her doom,
She languishes and dies, all petals in disclose;

Thus, in the very blossoming of thy youthfulness,
When heaven and earth paid homage to thy loveliness,
Fate cut thee down, as ash of rose-leaves to repose.

As fit funereal gifts, take thou these tears of mine,
And take these blossoms and this urn of milk as thine,
That thus, alive and dead, thine essence be but rose.

TO CLARK ASHTON SMITH

(13 January 1893–14 August 1961)

One with the stars and singing splendor of the night,
The alchemist of beauty and of bale is gone,
Leaving at last in long-delayed and stately flight
For worlds where never-ending suns of wonder dawn;
Where unicorned chimaeras all of crystal fawn
About the breast of sphinx and succubus asmile;
Where black, profulgent prodigies of horror spawn,
Alone or through the cunning necromantic guile
Of mighty and omniscient mages; where the vial
Of darkly glamorous night has poured its black above
Some Atlantean, enchanted, ocean-foundering isle
Where prince and princess prove the philtre-spell of
    love. . . .

One with all worlds and things of wonder
    lying lost of space and time,
He is at long last gone to claim,
    once more, his native sphere sublime.

August & December 1961.

PAVANE

Upon hearing the Pavane *of Messire Gabriel Fauré.*

Where proud imperial peacocks pomp their many-pomped pavane,
Their stately dance of splendor pavonine,
And where courtier and courtezan
Mingle amid and mock those pomps of peacock eyne,
There the plenilune pours forth her flood of silence opaline
Within an inmost woodland glade,
While pipes of Pan combine
A poignant note of darkling light and lambent shade,
Of fingers yielding half-afraid,
As fingers touch and linger and then lightly pass
Within an inmost woodland glade
Of muted evergreen and muted gold-green grass,
Where courtier and courtezan,
And proud imperial peacocks pomp a many-pomped and many-hued
                    pavane.

WHEN WE WERE PRINCE AND PRINCESS

Translated from the Atlantean of King Atlantarion I.

When we were prince and princess deep in deepest love,
And roamed we at our will on Atlantean isles,
What deep delight to prove the philtre-spells of love!

The spells, the charms, the shy enchantments of our smiles,
And then the pulse of love within our hearts would rise,
Would put to lingering flight our shyness and our smiles. . . .

In secrecy we would dare love's great enterprise,
Its incandescent spells of passion, pain, and throe,
That proudly blazed the shield of love's great enterprise. . . .

But spell of spells of all those spells of long ago,
That last brief spell of splendor and of ecstasy,
When we were prince and princess oh so very long ago. . . .

And though our love, our names, in future cycles none
        May know and call to memory,
We shall not care, for once we were together one
        With splendor and eternity.

THE CROWN AND TRIDENT

Translated from the Atlantean of King Atlantarion I.

". . . And here, in the centremost heart of that immense, marvellous, and imperial city, Mount Atlantis, the Acropolis, like a first Olympus, soared eternally into the air. . . ."

By Michel de Labretagne, from *Le roman de la
princesse Aïs et du prince Atlantaryon.*

High noon, and on this cloudless day how bright
The sun upon the arch Acropolis
From lowest slopes up to its utmost height;
From colonnades, towers, temples, palaces,
Fine-etched like sacrificial chalices,
To where a crown and trident huge aspires
To utmost—empyrean—synthesis;
To where the white-gold breath of sun conspires
With orichalch the most resplendent fires,
And where atop the mountain's mass of granite
Attains no sound of fanfares, flutes, and lyres,
Only the wandering notes of star and planet. . . .

Only this coin with crown and trident stamped in gold
Remains to speak the high-spired splendidness of old.

SONG

Translated from the Atlantean of Athallarion.

O ebon-colored rose,
How much too darkly do you bloom!
Abyssal night bestows,
As from some vast, unlighted tomb,
Its utter black, its utter gloom,
Upon your stem, your foliage, and your face,
Your face wherefrom pours forth perfume,
A dark perfume . . . of pure and perfect grace. . . .
O aura fit for him that would have Death's embrace!

"THY SPIRIT WALKS THE SEA"

Dedicated to Nora May French, in memoriam.

"What shifting films of distance fold you, blind you,
    This windy eve of dreams, I cannot tell.
I know they grope through some strange mist to find you,
    My hands that give you Greeting and Farewell."
                              Nora May French, *Ave Atque Vale.*

Standing upon this Lesbian promontory
Which rises up beside the western sea,
We muse on Phyllis and her Sapphic glory:
Since that same time when you but seemed to flee
And in these waves they cast your ashes free,
Now more than half a hundred years have passed:
Beyond this world, its impure grief and glee,
You hold a greater world . . . the ocean's vast . . .
With whose untrammeled realms your spirit shall outlast:

Within what sunken colonnades and gardens do you roam,
Amid what palaces of some deep Atlantean past? . . .
Whose regal ways you have returned to claim once more as home:

And have you found—beyond this planet's barriers and bars—
Those greater spheres and realms . . . deep in the Ocean Sea of stars?

Point Lobos: 31 December 1968.

RECOMPENSE

Translated from the Atlantean of an unknown poet.

"All that the sea has taken, the sea restores:"
                              Clark Ashton Smith, *Sea Cycle.*

The fabled wealth of the Atlantean kings,
Within the muck and slime of the ocean-floor,
Lies far below with lost, forgotten things:
And can it be no splendor shall restore
The treasures of Atlantis that of yore
Her subject kings and queens in tribute gave?
The sunset and the sunrise evermore,
With gorgeousness extravagantly brave,
Invoke her stores of gold out from her vast sea-grave:

And in the twilight after sunset or before the morn—
Within the great, unending robe woven of many a wave—
The archimperial purple of Atlantis is reborn:

And in the night the white-gold stars that vibrate in the sea
Now hold her wealth of silver and of pale flame-gold in fee.

TO A YOUTH

Whether in some palaestra of old Greece,
Your body nude, bronzed, glistening all with oil;
Or whether questing for some Golden Fleece,
A golden warrior in some Jason's toil;
Or whether through the Forum's noise and moil,
You passed, dressed in your noble *tunica;*
Or whether decked with ruff and pearls and foil,
You pomped within the court of Henri III,
The pampered and befeathered minion of a De Valois. . . .

Or whether now, with golden body blazoned on the sun,
Surfing before the breaking wave with fierce, divine *éclat,*
O cavalier of the sea, now, when you and the sea are one. . . .

With mouth and eyes of mingled rapture and of mingled ruth,
Ever were you—and will you be—the same, O golden youth.

SPENSERIAN STANZA-SONNET EMPOURPRÉ

"Strange pleasures are known to him who flaunts the immarcescible purple of poetry before the color-blind."

Clark Ashton Smith, *The Black Book.*

As if they waxed in Eden's garden-close;—
The iris, and the orchid, and the lyre;
The peacock, and the poppy, and the rose;
The phoenix, and his death and birth in fire;
The amaranth; the nenuphar; the choir,
Ere dawn, of little birds; the unicorn;
Amber, and ambergris; purple from Tyre;
The lover by his lover-lass forlorn;—
Thus, all things "rich and strange" it seems are now forsworn:

But natheless I shall sing them in my minor mode,
The runes intoned by some faint otherworldly horn,
The melodies far-wafted from the antipode:

For such—the peacock, and the poppy, and the rose—
Still wax within some dim Aidennic garden-close.

A SYMBOL FOR ALL SPLENDOR LOST

"Abides nor goal nor ultimate of peace,
  Nor lifts a beacon on the cosmic deep
    To guide our wandering world on seas sublime . . ."
                    George Sterling, *Sonnets by the Night Sea:* I.

No more, no less than Plato's quaint conceit,—
Atlantis,—more than myth, this memory
Of a paradise we may once more complete,
This image of an island empery
Supreme in wealth, extent, antiquity,—
Has now become my own arcanic lore,
But more, a torch deep in eternity,
A symbol for all splendor lost, and more,
A sign for all of loveliness evanished evermore. . . .

Forevermore? Perhaps there shall rise yet in far-off time,—
Beyond this bleak, blind interim of now and nevermore,—
Many a new Atlantis from "the cosmic sea sublime". . . .

And there, perhaps, in future gardens marvellous and vast,
Shall bloom again all splendor and all beauty lost and past.

THE ASHES IN THE ROSE GARDEN

Dedicated to B. M. B., 1885–1965, in memoriam;
whose ashes lie buried in the Rose Garden of
Mountain View Cemetery, Oakland, California.

The chateau by the chatelaine
         is now, alas! forlorn:
But for her, thus, a new domain,
A realm of rose, and through the rose
         her essence is reborn:
For her the air, the sun, the rain;
For her the rose that shall remain;
The bud, the rose, the bud again;
And for her, thus, a new domain,—
Of dreams, and doubtful roses,
         in a fabled garden-close;
Of trouvère and fair chatelaine;
Of lovely antique tapestries,
         and gracious dim repose. . . .
Farewell, farewell, and thrice farewell,
         our lovely gracious lady all of rose.

TO EDMUND SPENSER

(1552?–1599)

". . . The Prince of Poets in his tyme . . ."
From the inscription on the monument to Spenser in Westminster Abbey.

Historiographers have said you died,
And were within Westminster Abbey laid
To rest—surely such worthies must have lied;
For at your seeming death you were conveyed,
While yet in courtly ruff and garb arrayed,
To Faeryland, and to Cleopolis,
That capital resplendently displayed,
And to the heart of that metropolis,—
Panthèa,—the city's crown, and proud acropolis:

And there, within that crystal tower-palace's great hall,
The place of Gloriana's court, the one true Bowre of Bliss;
You have completed your great song, O gentlest bard of all:

Now rightly as *Sir* Edmund Spenser may you there be seen,
Both knight and poet laureate to Her Majesty, the Queene.

ROSE VERDASTRE

Translated from the Atlantean of Athallarion.

". . . And so they laid the queen to rest in her own garden-close. . . ."
By the Prince Atlantarion,
from the *Minor Chronicles of Atlantis.*

We wandered where the greenish roses grow
Close-gathered in the garden of a queen
Dead long ago from jealous love and woe:
Her jealous heart hath bred those roses green
And yellow-green whose phosphorescent sheen
Relumes the phosphors of her sepulchre:
Dire thorns, enormous and verdazurine,
Nourished from roots that subtly disinter,
Revive the piercing spites and jealousies that were:

The roses' fleshlike faces, velvet-soft, assume
Weird glamors gangrenous, whilst they administer
An overwhelming tide of strangely lush perfume:

We turned, our heart replete with jealous love and woe,
And wandered on from where those greenish roses grow.

AVE ATQUE VALE

Dedicated to R. G. P., in remembrance of March 1961.

Now, through the endless, void, and vastly halls of night,
The moon proceeds along her star-emblazoned way,
And pours deep in my heart her plenitude of light,
As in a Gothic hall, alone and old and gray:
Through shattered vaults, the reflex of a far-off day
Descends, and casts in ghostly wise a white-gold glow
On symbols of past loves, and comes at length to play
Upon a portrait I forevermore shall know,
The moon-bright likeness of the one so loved so long ago. . . .

Behold the gold flame of the mouth, the splendid body bare,
The face with beauty and with youth divinely all aglow,
The sea-green eyes, the gold-flushed skin, the darkling sea-gold hair:

Thus, hail and, thus, farewell to one who never shall return—
Although the flambeaux of the stars in unending vigils burn.

THAÏS AND ALEXANDER IN PERSEPOLIS

Dedicated to José-Maria de Heredia, in memoriam.

Beneath the stars' impassive scrutiny they pause,
Outside the Apadana's western colonnade;
The villaged plain below—from garden, field, and glade—
Still wafts forth homage to the empery that was.

And everywhere but here—with laughter, song, applause—
The torch-lit, drunk, triumphant revellers parade;
But here, where destiny now is weighed and counterweighed,
Silence . . . while thought of retribution gnaws and gnaws.

Outlined against the splendent portico they stand,
Each richly robed, each with a gold wine-cup in hand:
She lifts her gaze towards him acclaimed of many fames. . . .

And the god-king observes with wonder and surmise
How, kindled by the Persian flambeau-fires, there flames
A splendor of destruction deep within her eyes.

A FRAGMENT

Translated from the Atlantean of an unknown poet.

The flame-red sun was made a paling moon by mist
As by the Ocean Sea we stood and mused at dawn
And watched the ghostly waves uproll from out the east:
Fashioned of mist, fantastical creatures came to fawn
About our feet, there in that half-light of the dawn,
Bearing us gifts of shadowy crowns and shadowy gems:
Anon tall kings and queens with faces proud and wan,
With strange lights pouring from their crystal diadems,
Filed slowly by, dressed in great purple robes with white-gold hems:

Tridents upon their crowns and in their hands they bore—
Of orichalch the teeth, of orichalch the stems—
While winds blew fanfares for them as they paced the shore:

More and more thickly swarmed the mist billowing out of the east,
And more fantastical grew the shapes created by the mist. . . .

O FAIR DARK EYES, O GLANCES TURNED ASIDE

Translated from the French of Louise Labé.

O fair dark eyes, O glances turned aside,
O ardent sighs, O tears poured forth in pain,
O endless nights whose vigils proved in vain,
O lustrous days whose charm did not abide;

O sad complaints, O obstinate desires,
O wasted time, O pains and pangs and cares,
O thousand deaths hid in a thousand snares,
O burning ills as of a thousand fires!

O mouth, O face, O hair, arms, hands, and fingers;
O plaintive lute, O voice that mournfully lingers;
So many flames to set a lass on fire!

Of thee I plain: for all the fires I bear,
For all that everywhere my heart I wear,
There has flown onto thee not one spark of desire.

THE CYDNUS

Translated from the French of José-Maria de Heredia.

Upon the darkling stream, within the sunset's blaze,
The purple and the white of the silver trireme loom;
Above her wake there trails a censer-borne perfume,
With flaffing of silken sails, with song of flute that strays.

Within the dazzling prow where Egypt's hawk displays,
Outside her royal dais, her glamor in utmost bloom,
Queen Cleopatra stands where sunset-lights illume,—
A great golden bird of prey with keen, attendant gaze.

Here rises Tarsus, where the disarmed warrior waits;
And in the enchanted air the enchantress elevates
Her amber arms that now the purple stains with rose;

She has not seen or sensed,—she has not felt Their breath,—
Beside her, scattering roses on the dark that flows,
The two Child-Gods: one is Desire, and one is Death.

GOLDEN MYCENAE

Citadel of gold and Cyclopean stone:
This proud lion couchant curled upon his dais,
With the mountains to the north as his great throne,
Southward sempiternally has fixed his face,
Gazing out across the sun-emblazoned space
Of the plains of Argos towards the sea's dark wine;
Patiently still searching for his golden race—
His first race of gods and godlike men—whose line
Blossomed, and then vanished . . . it would seem to no Design. . . .

It may be that no splendor passes evermore from Earth,
But that, through endless incantations—subtle, strange, divine—
It knows in far-off time and space a new resplendent birth:

In what age, in what world, shall this proud lion find again—
Deep in the sea of stars—his race of gods and godlike men?

LULLABY

Translated from the Atlantean of Prince Atlantarion.

Here, where the earth and sea meet evermore,
And Mother Night takes all within her keep,
The waves wash quietly upon the shore:
The wild and white-maned horses of the deep
Have all been stabled, and are now asleep
Far down below where sunken triremes lie:
Above the shore, the sea-birds soar and sweep,
And through the trees that rise upon the sky,
A cool, soft sea-wind plays an old, old lullaby.

MINOR CHRONICLES OF ATLANTIS

Translated from the Atlantean of Prince Atlantarion.

Dedicated to Fritz and Jonquil Leiber.

PROEM

"Many and varied and curious were the stories, the histories, the miscellanea related by the poet Aon to the princess Aïs, during the time that they were sailing aboard the quinquireme of the Archking's eldest brother, the Grand Archknight Prince Anorthys, as the great ship was making her way across the eastern expanses of the Ocean Sea, and westward to Atlantis from the princess's native land located on, as well as to the south of, the shores of Ylliphya, in the very north of Iffrikonn.

"Aon told the princess of quaint and fabulous monsters like the hippokampos; of the river Amphus that waters the Great Vale of Atlantis; of the delta of the Amphus and the seven principal streams thereof; of the gigantic nenuphars that blossom upon her waters; of the shape of the Archkingdom and the significance thereof; of the strange obelisks of Atlantis that line her metropolitan streets; of the loves and the sorrows and the deaths of olden lovers. Of these, and many other things, the poet descanted, to the delight or the wonder or the horror or the bafflement or the edification of the princess."

By Michel de Labretagne, from *Le roman de la princesse Aïs et du prince Atlantaryon.*

THE HIPPOKAMP

High above the Ocean Sea weaving and reweaving her boundless tapestry of ever-cresting waves, within the prow of the great quinquireme ablaze with the late-afternoon sun, and just behind the huge heraldic sea-horse that crowns the stem, two figures are seated on a couch of ebony inlaid with silver and pale flame-gold. They look out over the westering sea.

One figure, attired in flowing scarves of violescent gauze, is the poet Aon, with his eyes green as the green of shoaling seas, and with his long and abundant mane of darkling sea-gold hair.

The other figure, to his right, is the princess Aïs, with her eyes blue like the azure of a tropical sky. Framed by her luxurious night-black hair that falls below her hams, and gowned in a simple flowing robe of green, she is leaning on a pile of iridescent cushions and fabrics.

Behind the couch rises up an enormous and purely ornamental zaör, the Atlantean harp and lyre, painted with a black, dimly refulgent lacquer, and strung with strings of a silver-seeming metal. The wind, sounding through the strings and within the hollowed body of the zaör, creates faint and bizarre sonorities.

Aon picks up from his left his great zaör of ebony strung with orichalch, and places it lovingly in his lap as though holding a child or a mistress. He shakes his great mane of hair, and strikes three ascending chords. He turns to Aïs, and gazes deep within her eyes. She looks back at her poet-mentor with serene attention and expectancy. They smile; and then Aon chants in his vibrant and sensitive tenor-voice.

"O Princess, although born an outlander, you have long known, from earliest childhood, I am sure, that all Atlantean ships—whether great or small, whether official or unofficial, whether for the transport of merchandise or of passengers—bear each upon their single or central rectangular sail an immense crown and trident woven in silhouette, just as this quinquireme bears one upon her own flame-colored central sail. . . . But enough of the crown and trident! I have sung that song enough. For the nonce I shall sing the song of the hippokamp."

He pauses and looks out over the westering sea, then points briefly to the huge sculpture at the summit of the prow, and then chants again but in an alien, deep, and hollow voice.

I

I am the hippokamp, or hippokampos, the sea-horse. Just as the crown and trident figures as the basic heraldic image, even so do I serve as the basic heraldic beast throughout the Empire of Atlantis, from the far north to the far south, from the far east to the far west.

Like most heraldic animals, I am—of course—a composite beast at best. The great Aÿsius created me three thousand years agone . . . Aÿsius, the chief court architect and sculptor during the reign of Poseidon III, called variously the Empire-Builder, the Earth-Shaker, and the First Lord of Sea and Land, amongst many another appellation.

Aÿsius had been seeking far and wide . . . to find a symbol for the dominion of many waters embodied in the Empire of Atlantis . . . and through that symbol an image for the very Ocean Sea herself.

Within these high seas, these great white-crested waves, or to use the traditional Atlantean figure of speech, these wild and white-maned horses of the deep, through which we are now sailing westward, he first discovered the idea of me.

Then he sought to find an avatar in which to render me concrete. From the land-horse he gave me my head, my neck, and my mane. From the little sea-horse that lives in tropical and semi-tropical seas, he gave me my body and my tail, magnifying both to monumental size.

Look how superbiously the long mane of the land-horse flows down over my neck and my back! Look how pertly the small fan-shaped fin of the little sea-horse is displayed at the bottom of my back and at the beginning of my tail!

But my tail—how pleased I am by that! My tail is longer and thicker and wider than that of the little sea-horse. It divides at the end into two proud fins which thrust out at right angles to the tail, and which are fashioned like those of leviathan, or of the veridical or actual sea-horse.

Gradually tapering towards the outer end, my tail curls back down towards my body, and thus into itself, shell-wise.

Whether hewn from granite or malachite or marble, or whether carven from rosewood or ebony or cypress, or whether cast entirely in bronze, in silver or in gold, or in the pale flame-gold of orichalch, I flaunt my imperious and imperial beauty everywhere.

Rampantly perched upon high rectangular pedestals, often with jewelled eyes whose dark profounds hide an unknown and unknowable fire, I proclaim the image of myself in vasty numbers throughout the Empire of Atlantis. Uncounted and uncountable is the population of my kind.

Eternal souvenir of the Ocean Sea, I rear up in gardens or in desert-wastes, I keep guard on either side of the thrones of kings, I stand in avenues within temples and palaces as well as without, I pleasantly disturb the monotony of long colonnades, or I piquantly cap the corners where two or more streets merge or pass through each other.

Or often I appear featured as the very figurehead itself on the summit of some ship's prow, just as I sit here crowning the stem of this quinquireme. Rather like large quizzical eyebrows forever arched in metaphysical doubt, inquiry, or speculation, my fanciful shape in bas-relief is emblazoned on either side of the stem on virtually all Atlantean ships, just above the huge eyes which, carven and painted, peer out over the unceasing waves.

Oftentimes I may seem wild and fierce, with my neck triumphantly arched, with my mouth agape, with my nostrils flared, and with my proud, regal, and abundant mane tossed madly about. But at other times I assume a mien calm and majestical, as befits a beast so frequently found at the ancient courts of kings.

I have lived in every time and clime of the Great Imperial Age that began three thousand years agone. For three thousand years my nostrils have respired exotic and opulent perfumes, the sweet and lethal breath of autumnal or vernal flowers, and the winds and vapors of manifold oceans.

For three thousand years my ears have resounded to the sophisticated

jargon of courtiers, the aggressive and competitive sibilance of merchants and merchant-princes, the cryptic utterances of sages and prophets, the mystic poetry of philosophers and metaphysicians, the clouded
lore of mysteriarchs, the music sublime of poets, the whispers and rap-
tures of lovers, and the imperious discourse of kings and prelates.

For three thousand years my stoned and implacable gaze has testified
to the pageant of an empire transpiring through the sovereign alkahest
of time. I know the history of imperial Atlantis at first sight and sound
and smell—whether originating in the marketplace or the temple or the
court—and just as well I know much never chronicled by the royal or
archroyal historiographers. And I shall outlast until the dis-solution of
that pageant, so long as one piece of Atlantean earth looms yet above
the waves.

Oddly but characteristically, poets and visionaries claim to have seen
me—in all veridicality—as early as the great Aÿsius had unveiled the
first carven example of myself. And since I am the quintessence of these
great white-crested waves, I would say that they have seen me for a fact,
and moreover on innumerable occasions.

Although I am a composite beast at best, I have had many another
heraldic animal patterned after me, the taurokamp, the leokamp, the sea-
satyr, the unicorned sea-horse, as well as the giant sea-scorpion. I am the
hippokamp, or hippokampos, the sea-horse.

II

I, too, am the hippokamp, or hippokampos, the sea-horse. But
whereas my brother hippokamp, the heraldic beast fashioned in substances multifarious, exists only through the medium of the mind of
man and only through the means afforded by his hand; I am the veridical and actual hippokamp, even though the numbers of my kind have
dwindled almost to the point of extinction.

Alas! as the Empire of Atlantis and her commerce have increased, so
has my species decreased in the over-all total of our far-flung population. And great is the pity and the pain of this fact, for we are a choice
and strangely beautiful animal.

Prone to wandering like the whale, we range all the way from the equatorial seas to the seas of the far north or of the far south. Peaceable and shy, we live in those places usually inaccessible to men and to the ships of men.

By preference as well as by olden tradition, we inhabit those areas where the sea and the land meet in an ever-changing welter of tides and currents and winds . . . raving and roaring around sea-caves and shelving sea-cliffs . . . and in and around the weirdly sculptured rocks of great sea-labyrinths.

Like the leviathan, we are a mammal and have evolved from the land-horse over a period of manifold aeons, and thus we still bear many points of resemblance to our brother species.

Our eyes, protected and encircled by thick protuberant muscles, project out from our head. Some small distance back from our eyes, our ears rise up, now hardly more than low vestigial cones.

Our mouth, too, has changed, for in adjusting to our new diet of sea-weed and sea-flower, mollusk and crustacean and fish, our upper and lower sets of teeth have metamorphosed into continuous ridges of an extra-sharp and extra-hard enamel-covered bone.

Our neck has become even thicker than that of the land-horse. Between the eyes and the ears, and a little bit back from the eyes, there lifts up a low serrulate crest which runs down the back of our neck and then disappears into the skin of our upper back.

The girth of our chest is considerable and exceeds even that of the great bull; like the leviathan, we can submerge for extended periods of time deep within the exquisite oblivion of Mother Ocean.

Our front legs, thick and short, have developed semi-prehensile appendages; our hind legs now form part of our long and sinuous tail which, muscular and supple, has thickened to such a degree that at the widest it easily equals our neck in girth.

Our tail rapidly tapers towards the outer end, and the tail's end itself, consisting of two fins issuing at right angles to the tail, we employ in the same way that the helmsman employs the rudder on one of your great Atlantean ships, to guide and govern the course.

And we have no pelt—only a thick, smooth, rubbery skin like that of the whale, and gray-green in hue, rather like the dull-toned, gray-green patina that forms on bronze and on brass, as well as on the darker, more copper-laden orichalchums.

Rarely will you witness us now, rarely do we let a man or a woman or a child behold us; just often enough so that mankind shall know for a verity that we still exist, even though we are, alas! gradually becoming a legendary and a mythical creature.

And though we make love with a passion, a fury, and an ingenuity that have no parallel or equal, our sea-dams hardly ever conceive any-more. And on those rare occasions when one of our females does give birth to a sea-foal who is perfect and who does not perish from the manifold hazards of our existence, supreme is our joyance and our de-light.

And then supreme is the joyance and the delight, the fervor and the freshness with which we, the sea-studs, can once more mount our sea-dams, hoping that the fruit from our labor of love shall also prove more than a momentary exaltation of the senses.

In the late afternoon the sea-studs and the sea-dams will court each other and then pair-off. Then as the sun's fierce disk of rubescent gold sinks and sets in the far west, we will join and, thus united, we will dive into the upper levels of the sea stained with the flames of sunset.

Then as the dusk of evening changes the upper sea into one enormous dark-gray pearl, we glide into those lower levels of twilight. Then as twilight passes into night, we descend still further, and roam those yet nether regions of eternal night. Thus deep within that womb of waters, and secure from all pursuit, we make love while Mother Ocean caresses us with her pervasive and inexorable affection.

Then after seemingly unending hours of making love—when we have lost all sense of time and space and self, when we can no longer distin-guish the night of waters from the night of stars, and when the dusk before dawn has once more changed the upper sea into one enormous dark-gray pearl—we reach our final and supreme climax.

Still united, after that little death which is love's ecstatic finish, we once more swim gradually towards the upper sea, and away from those regions of death and love and eternal night. At last, in the midst of waves aflame with the incandescent gold of sunrise, we once more break through the surface of the upper sea. Then, with a strange awe and rapture commingled of lingering ecstasy and prescient sorrow, we part and then swim on upon our individual ways.

But sooner or later, after the due passage of time, when no little seahorse finally succeeds our amatory labor, then we make love once more with our tragic and wonted irony. And surely, because of this, we have become a sad and sorrowful species, and the warm salty tears that we weep are now more of grief than of joy, and immingle easily with the greater salt and the greater grief of Mother Ocean.

My brother hippokamp, no disrespect nor less love to him for this, is an illusion, a pretty piece of heraldic imagery, but he cannot ever become extinct. Having never truly lived, never can he truly die. Do not forget me, however, for I am alive. Do not consign my species to the realms of myth and legend yet. Remember me. I, too, am the hippokamp, or hippokampos, the sea-horse.

THE ALPHA HUGE

". . . Shaped like as an alpha huge. . . ."
Old Atlantean Figure of Speech

A sacred mark of the most profound significance, featured extensively
in the older imperial heraldry, the alpha huge has discovered its most
monumental expression in the shape of the Archkingdom: A shape
which may find abstraction in the figure of a tall isosceles triangle of
which the two long sides project a little bit below the base, this design
usually in an equal mix of or and vert and on a field azure: Thus, the
Archkingdom with the massive prongs of her three great land's-ends,—
southeast, southwest, and north,—lying athwart the great blue shield of
the Ocean Sea. For principles arcane as well as practical, the alpha huge
is the first glyph in the official alphabet of imperial Atlantis as created
by—as well as at the behest of—the First Lord of Sea and Land, Poseidon III.

From furthest eld, speaking as the result of a wisdom both sublime
and occult, seers and mysteriarchs have averred that the alpha huge is a
sign descended from Earth's prime as well as a sign to represent or envi-
sion somehow the same. A symbol for the vernal paradise, the world in
the first flowering of existence, as well as a symbol for the autumnal
paradise, the world that has grown old and that waxes towards the inevitable decline, a world such as Atlantis, alas!—this image adumbrates
also the beginning of creation as well as the mysteries of the further
prime.

A sacred mark of the most profound significance, the alpha huge—
according to the revelations of yore—shall emerge again but only in
the latter cycles just before the end, to remind and reassure the soul
prophetic of the inevitable birth or rebirth which always lies beyond that
final death of all things.

THE RIVER CALLED AMPHUS

The great river-system . . . the Amphus . . . watering the very heart it-self of the island continent which is the Archkingdom . . . begins in the springs and streams and rills fed by the eternal snows crowning the alti-tudinous mountains that surround the Vale of Mythnom . . . north of the great mountain-heart-land Poseidonis . . . cradled by the clouds and by the sky . . . where the snow-like clouds and the snow-clad mountains are one to the distant eye of vision. . . .

Descending the sharply decadent slopes of the mountains . . . the brooks and streams . . . soon on the floor of Mythnom-Vale . . . intone their way into the little rivers, into the pools and lakes and ponds, into the interconnecting canals . . . all these in turn ultimately playing forth into the valley-centered and southward-streaming Monamphus . . . past the myriad farms and estates, past the innumerable houseboats and float-ing palaces, past the woods and orchards and parks. . . . The high garden-valley canal-world of Mythnom-Vale . . . the Great Garden in the Sky. . . .

Now the southern end of Mythnom-Vale . . . the Monamphus divides her solemn hymn at the great city At-Tho-Then . . . descending down into the great mountain-heart-land Poseidonis . . . as the eastern and western branches of the Poämphus . . . flowing south through the Great Vale to-East and the Great Vale to-West that lie between the three great ranges of the sky-cleaving Eiphlox Mountains. . . . And in the Great Vale to-East, on both sides of the eastern Poämphus midmost, the great city Zaära . . . and in the Great Vale to-West, on both sides of the western Poämphus midmost, the great city Zhaärth. . . .

In turn the western and the eastern branches of the Poämphus gather into the great lake . . . the Gates of Day . . . to the east of the Outhanox, the Great Citadel of Poseidonis, and to the east of the attendant great city Xonorr just north of the ancient fortress . . . and the lake, the for-tress, and the city . . . all this lies at the foot of the southernmost moun-tains of the great central Eiphlox range. . . .

Now the waters of the great lake descend southward in spectacular fountains and waterfalls ... down over a gradual series of ever-widening terraces ... the Steps of Day ... with peculiar out-jutting rocks eroded by the ever-falling waters into bizarre and often colossal shapes ... with towered isles crowned by lush and turreted greenery, and fraught with strange vivid blooms.... Now the upper and northernmost floor of the Great Vale of Atlantis.... The great flood of waters ... as the eastern branch of the Amphus proper ... pursues an eastward-projecting concave-course ... rushing past the paralleling eastern mountain-girdle of the Great Vale of Atlantis....

Meanwhile, to the west, and separated by a wide ridge of ruinous rock interspersed with copses of dark tall trees ... the great Lake Yllthyrrya ... fed by natural subterranean tunnels that accumulate the considerable seepage from the western Poämphus high above the tunnels, and just to the north of the great lake ... from Yllthyrrya flows the western branch of the Amphus proper ... pursuing an inversely similar course to that of the eastern Amphus....

Between these two major branches of the Amphus ... the vast sea of verdure called the Great Vale of Atlantis ... the great grainery that feeds an Empire ... crisscrossed with canals for irrigation and navigation ... cinctured by mountains and by hills on all sides ... from the rich alluvial soil the farmers mine the opulent and multi-varied gold of cereal-grains both summer and winter.... On the eastern bank of the western Amphus midmost, the great city Izzarth ... on the western bank of the eastern Amphus midmost, the great city Sfarnyx.... At last, at the southern and lowermost part of this greatest of valleys, the eastern Amphus and the western Amphus gather into the vast Lake of Lotus choked with water-lilies ... upon the southern marge of the lake, the Ampheum, the great fane to and of the Amphus, adumbrates her massy outlines from amidst her environing verdure....

At last the southern midmost marge of the island continent which is the Archkingdom ... the great river called Amphus pushes down from the Lake of Lotus and through the low mountains and high hills of the coast ... facing the Ocean Sea to the south ... lavishly spreading out her delta shaped like a vast full-blown lotus ... a lotus like one of the manifold gigantic nenuphars that haunt the turgid waters of her mouth of seven mouths. . . .

Between the two midmost streams of the Amphus delta and close to the Ocean Sea . . . the great imperial seat Atlantis the City . . . the capital of Atlantis the Archkingdom as well as of the Empire of Atlantis . . . and thus chief of the seven great cities located within the island continent. . . . At last, like a huge and multi-coiled serpent with one enormous head of manifold mouths, the Amphus disgorges her abundance of dust and dirt and detritus into the ever-attendant waters of Mother Ocean . . . thus immingling her streams with that greater flux which has no end and no beginning. . . .

But in time some of these identical particles of water, some soon, some later, rise up from that great flux yclept Mother Ocean but in the form of manifold vapors that pass up into the clouds far overhead. . . . And in time some of these clouds moving northward over the Great Vale of Atlantis change into rains that fall lightly or precipitously down upon and into the land. . . . Other clouds moving further northward change into blizzards or caresses of snow, to coronate with dazzling splendors the mountain-peaks of that great mountain-heart-land Poseidonis or, yet further north, the peaks of the altitudinous mountains that surround the Vale of Mythnom . . . cradled by the clouds and by the sky . . . where the snow-like clouds and the snow-clad mountains are one to the distant eye of vision. . . . And thus those particles of water turn and return in that cycle of cycles which never can have an end and which never can have a beginning. . . .

THE AMPHUS DELTA

"Alpha, Delta Plane and in the Round, and Three."
Old Nonsense Jingle of Atlantis.

Shaped like a vast full-blown lotus as observed in silhouette, the delta of the great river called Amphus hath seven principal streams. From west to east these are by name: the Alphis, the Aälphis, the Amnaältis, the Amphorial, the Amphamar, and flowing southeast from the Amphamar half-way down her course, the Ataämphus, and finally the Alphessys. Between the two midmost streams, the Amnaältis and the Amphorial, the great imperial capital Atlantis respendently displays the vast circle of her megalopolis.

The old nonsense jingle which virtually all Atlanteans will utter ever and anon, often irrelevantly, it would seem, is facile enough to explicate. The alpha—of course—refers to the Archkingdom, the delta plane to the delta of the Amphus, the delta in the round to the towered cone of Mount Atlantis, the Acropolis, arising from the centremost heart of the great capital city, and the three refers to the trident on the huge crown and trident atop the apex of the Acropolis. Thus, the main or concrete level of meaning, but there are others . . . of course . . . as always . . . .

Upon the delta's bayous, upon her marshes and pools and ponds, wherever and whenever the river-waters run quietly, the broad flat leaves and the deep, broad, and multi-petalled cups of the manifold gigantic nenuphars blossom forth, revealing their simple but still cryptic signs to any and all who may care to look . . . sometimes in the sunlight, sometimes in the shade, crimson or white or yellow or blue or purple . . . or, rarest and most beautiful of all, the giant black lotus. . . .

THE IMPERIAL CROWN JEWELS OF ATLANTIS

Mount Atlantis, the Acropolis of Atlantis the City, and the arch Acropolis in all the Empire of Atlantis! Close to the Ocean Sea, and between the two midmost streams of the Amphus delta, the Amnaältis and the Amphorial, the great imperial capital Atlantis resplendently displays the vast circle of her megalopolis. From within the third and innermost ring of the three great harbors, or rings of water, that lie concentred thus at the very heart of the city . . . there lifts up the towered cone of the arch Acropolis . . . completely surrounded by the great Sacred Grove planted by Poseidon III three thousand years agone. . . .

Mount Atlantis! O Empire's heart piling relentlessly up towards the heavens . . . O high-spiring crown soaring over fifteen-hundred imperial feet into the air . . . O great aspiring mass of stone as much of marble now as originally of granite . . . O tremendous and constantly evolving conspiracy between man and nature . . . O huge treasury compact of Atlantean life and art and culture. . . .

Mount Atlantis! How much without! The great imperial terraces aflame with the royal blooms of rose and lily and poppy . . . the colonnades . . . the towers and turrets . . . the garden-bowers . . . the temples . . . the trees that rise in tall and royal assemblies on the middle and upper slopes . . . the palaces . . . the great portals with double doors . . . the great flying buttresses topped by sculptures of every description and of every enduring material . . . the great imperial staircases ascending from level to level . . . even to the very summit surmounted by the archroyal observatory. . . .

Mount Atlantis! Whether within the Acropolis . . . within the unending spaces hewn out of the living stone . . . or whether without . . . out upon the multi-leveled slopes of the mountain . . . are the great halls of state . . . the throne-halls . . . the banquet-halls . . . the treasuries . . . the gatherings and avenues of statues and other sculptures . . . the great jetting fountains . . . the pools and basins and waterfalls . . . the shrines of divinities manifold. . . .

Mount Atlantis! How much within! Housed within this huge trea-

sury are treasures beyond count . . . treasures that come from all over the
Empire and the world . . . treasures given as tribute for over three mi-
lennia by a grateful and worshipping people to their living deity, the
Archking, and through the sacred prism of his being, proffered thus to
Atlantis herself . . . but chief of these treasures are the imperial crown
jewels. . . .

But first and foremost of the ordinary treasures . . . the strange scrolls
inscribed with curious lore and perilous mysteries, and illuminated with
metallic inks and with precious feathers and metals and stones. . . . The
costly and exotic fabrics of subtle weave . . . cloth of silver . . . cloth of
gold . . . cloth of electrum . . . cloth of orichalch . . . cloth of copper for
lovely copper skins. . . . Tapestries and carpets created from furs or woven from choice fabric-threads in accordance to fantastical designs. . . .
Dyes rich and rare . . . the black ink manufactured by the giant squids of
Atatemthessys . . . the opulent red-purples of Murexidia . . . that easternmost realm bordering on the easternmost of the Seas Within . . . the
Seas Within the Gates of Gades. . . . The strange and endless minerals
teased into extra-ordinary shapes. . . . Giant urns and vases carven from
gigantic masses of cinnabar imported from the vast island kingdom of
Lemuria lying athwart the great tropical ocean south of Yndessys and
east of southeastern Iffrikonn. . . .

But the treasure of treasures are the imperial crown jewels of
Atlantis. . . . Pearls that still retain the cool and opalescent gloom of
Yndessessian seas. . . . Pomegranates with rind of beaten flame-gold and
with seeds of garnet. . . . Giant snowflakes chiseled from purest crystal.
. . . Madrepore from the far-western tropical seas that wash above the
sunken fields and plains of the monstrous and now lost continent of
Mu. . . . Coral red as the red wine of autumnal sunsets in Avalonessys.
. . . Coral white and candid as the candid white of the single wondrous
horn sported by the unicorn. . . . Amber . . . black amber . . . white
amber . . . as white as the opaque ice of old icicles frosted over. . . . Heraldic beasts hewn from uncommon minerals or cast entirely out of precious metals . . . silver unicorns . . . emblematical squids of lapis lazuli
. . . golden leokamps . . . giant sea-scorpions in tattooed and armored

mail of electrum-plates . . . amber taurokamps . . . Atlantillian jaguärs of malachite with bright polished eyes of yellow jasper . . . hippokamps of orichalchum . . . swans of roseate ivory with bills of black onyx. . . . Sceptres and maces and sceptre-staffs . . . almost all surmounted with crown and tridents. . . . And here and there and everywhere blaze out the manifold and variegated splendors of tridented crowns in substances multifarious . . . tridented crowns that have often sat heavy but always proud upon the heads and brows of many royal generations. . . .

But the most perfect and beautiful treasure of the imperial crown jewels . . . the crown and trident whose nine spikes form three individual tridents of which the bottom-pieces adhere to the wide brow-encircling band of the crown proper, thus making over-all a total of twelve teeth, the refulgent thorns of royalty and of divinity. . . . This type of crown and trident is usually made entirely of rare gem-stones fitted together with the finest pale flame-gold . . . a dazzle of light and weight. . . . This is the same as that huge crown and trident—fashioned of purest orichalchum—which crowns the great lanthorn or beacon which in turn roofs the central and highest edifice of the archroyal observatory which in turn arises from the highest heights of Mount Atlantis. . . . Here, at high noon, on a clear day, the sun and the pale flame-gold conspire to adumbrate certain ultimate splendors, and here still reach, however faintly, vagrant and random echoes of those greater harmonies created by the stars and planets and galaxies . . . in that orbiting and balancing which has no end and no beginning . . . the music of the perfect spheres moving through the pregnant emptiness of perfect space. . . .

THE ATLANTEAN OBELISK

Like the heraldic sea-horse, the peculiarly Atlantean, nine-sided, and always ithyphallic obelisk, a characteristic feature of Atlantean architecture, usually slightly tapered towards the upper end, and almost always topped with a crown and trident, will rear up virtually anywhere and everywhere . . . whether within sleeping chambers . . . on either side of the bed or couch . . . or whether within parks and gardens . . . rising up from the midst of the perennial roses or within the midst of the towering yews and crypresses with their proud aspiring shafts . . . or whether within temples and palaces or whether without . . . on either side of the thrones of kings or of gods . . . or whether within city-streets . . . along the wide thoroughfares of the great cities . . . especially within the great imperial capital Atlantis. . . .

The Atlantean obelisk, although thus used in a variety of ways, is above all featured in order to outline the great colonnaded city-streets . . . particularly during the long and star-bright or fog-tapestried vigils of the night . . . many obelisks are first surmounted with a tall effulgent lamp, or lanthorn, and are then surmounted with a crown and trident, and hence are yet one more type of common street-illumination. . . . Like the heraldic seahorse, the peculiarly Atlantean, nine-sided, and always ithyphallic obelisk will rear up virtually anywhere and everywhere . . . both expectedly and unexpectedly . . . .

THE GARDEN OF JEALOUS ROSES

This history happened shortly after the 1,001st-Year Jubilee of the Empire of Atlantis, during the reign of Atlas LII, called Ataquor, whose Queen Consort Archroyal was the Sovereign Lady Lillittis, belovèd over all. Anon, by some foul necromancy beyond precedent, a weird change came over the queen; from being a warm, compassionate, and loving person Lillittis became at irregular intervals imperious and haughty and hateful, to such an extent that the Archking and his people could only conclude that an ancient succubus, a monstrous persona from the black abyss of elder time, had somehow invaded the body of their queen and was desperately striving to win control. For all did mark the great jealousy that the new personality bore to the old one, and she to her, above all in regard to their individual amour for the Archking. In one thing alone did the two personalities acocrd: in their love and cultivation of the queen's rose-garden located in a garden-bower on the lower western slopes of Mount Atlantis and thus in the primordial twilight afforded by the great Sacred Grove.

In vain did the Archking summon the most celebrated necromancers and the most learnèd of doctors; in vain did the men of medicine administer to the queen their most renowned and reputedly efficacious potions and nostrums; and in vain did the mages perform their most potent spells and rituals of exorcism above and around the person of the Sovereign Lady. Gradually the struggle for domination between the two personalities enfeebled and then killed the queen, dead thus from jealous love and woe. But upon her death-bed, when she had once more become the warm, compassionate, and loving person whom everyone did love with such dearling regard, Queen Lillittis made her last and very last request, that her body be buried in her own garden-close, instead of being lapidified and then enthroned—according to the olden custom—within the funereal halls of the Outhanox, the Great Citadel of Poseidonis.

The Archking, acquiescent to his queen's dying request but bewildered and saddened beyond measure by these monstrous and sorrowful happenings, broke thus with the immemorial tradition, charging the grave and holy men of death to bury the body of Lillittis within a sepulchre just below those roses that she had nurtured with such care and with such rare accord, and so they laid the queen to rest in her own garden-close with the utmost of due funereal pomp.

But the roses growing above her body changed their wonted and variegated hues of red and white and orange and yellow to green and yellow-green, assuming a weird phosphorescence, and soon sporting enormous blue-green thorns. And their new fragrance was not as the fragrance of other roses—delicate and subtle—but was overwhelmingly luscious like the breath of the night-blossoming jasmine. And the people of the court and the city could only reach the lamentable conclusion that the same foul necromancy that had come upon the queen during life had now pursued her into death. And an even greater sorrow, mingled with terror and horror, fell upon the already grief-pierced hearts of the Archking and of his people . . . and the garden-close became shunned by all, except by poets and by other solitary lovers, often also jealous, who well understood the meaning and the bitter appeal of that thrice-accursed place. . . .

THE TALE OF AN OLDEN LOVE

In the little village of Noöm, just south of the metropolis At-Tho-Then, in the southernmost part of Mythnom-Vale, where the Monamphus divides her solemn hymn into the western and the eastern branches of the Poämphus, there lived with their families the maiden Lailis and the youth Ampara. Now this happened in the reign of Atlas LXXVII, called Naörthris, during the fifth century of the second milennium of the Atlantean Empire.

Playmates and friends from earliest childhood, Lailis and Ampara, upon attaining to middle adolescence, became something more than brother and sister to each other. They were standing by the eastern shore of the western Poämphus, in the pearl-gray dusk just before the morn, when they kissed for the first time as man and woman. With a trembling thrill, and with the dawning of fierce and incredible suns within their hearts, they realized that they loved each other but no longer as brother and sister. And a great fear and a great joy caught at their hearts. And they sank in each other's arms down upon a blossom-embroidered hillock; and so they made love there by the river, on the green turf, in the midst of the flowering trees, where the glories of the early morning sun found them thus at length.

Shortly thereafter, and alas for the lovers, they became separated: Lailis, by virtue of her great beauty, had been invited to the court of the Archking, to fulfill her novel offices as one of the archroyal concubines.

Ampara, overwhelmed with grief and carrying his bardic lute, wandered forth from Noöm, never to return; and simply wandering wherever life happened to lead him, he sang of his lost love with a poignant beauty, gratefully recreating his private pain into a royal pleasure for others. And people hearkened to his lyrics, and great became the rumor of Ampara's invocations, eternally calling back a goddess who has eternally departed. Anon, in the course of his wanderings, the lyric poet came to the imperial seat, Atlantis the City, the greatest of the seven great cities located within the island continent. Initiating himself into the artistic life of the City, Ampara gradually gained unique fame for the songs he sang, and the manner in which he sang them; and the arbiters of creative elegance gave him their official acceptance, pronouncing him a wandering poet of recognized genius.

Soon did Atlas Naörthris invite Ampara to sing for him and the imperial court. Lailis had by now become the favorite concubine of the Archroyal Majesty, and she alone of all those assembled in that great court knew of whom Ampara sang. Royally did the Archking and his court acclaim the poet, but the lovers, dissimulating their true feelings of mutual passion, smiled at each other with a strange and secret look understandable to none but themselves. And once again, as in some olden play of paradise and hell, there flamed within their hearts the dawning of fierce and incredible suns, and Lailis and Ampara knew then that their love had never died but had only smoldered until they could meet yet once again.

Their olden love thus revived, the lovers found ways and means to meet in privacy, and to plan a flight incognito from Atlantis the City. Disguised as wandering minstrels, they met one night at midnight in the plaza due south of Mount Atlantis, and crossed over the divers plaza-bridges and rings of land into the Outer City, going from there into the low mountains and high hills of the coast west of the City and the Amphus delta. And thus they fled the Atlantean court and capital. . . .

For three days and three nights of mad happiness, the lovers journeyed west, safe for awhile from any pursuit, receiving food and hospitality at isolated farms and villages, or eating from the abundance provided by a wild and fruitful nature. They travelled along the southern marge of the island continent, on roads rarely used but which led eventually to the little seaport of Aliddium that lay where the great prong of southwestern Atlantis joins the larger mass of land. From Aliddium the lovers were planning to win passage—by assuming the position of ship's minstrels—aboard some argosy of trade going to Atlantillia and thence to the Antillias. But they somehow became lost in a series of valleys running ever west.

On the fourth day Lailis and Ampara wandered into an ineffably lush-green valley fraught with such grand and umbrageous trees as they had never known or seen before; trees with enormous orchid-like flowers wherefrom poured forth strange and subtle aromas. . . . Anon, late in the day, just before the twilight yielded to the night, they discovered within a lowland a natural pool with a great jet in the middle thereof eternally rising and falling. Now the lovers, upon seeing these pure and crystal waters, felt a great thirst, and rapidly and unreflectingly they bent down and drank deep, noticing a curious metallic aftertaste which soon passed, however. Suddenly Ampara remembered old stories about a natural spring with attendant pool located somewhere in this general area . . . a spring whose waters did not give life but only took it away . . . the dread Fountain of Ddath. . . . But Ampara said nothing and only smiled.

Now the lovers felt an unwonted lassitude and then a black tide of mortal fatigue . . . swiftly and with great passion, Lailis and Ampara, somehow both suddenly understanding all, kissed and embraced each other . . . smiling tranquilly amid their soft and sudden tears, they perceived far within each other's eyes the ghostly renascence of fierce and incredible suns . . . and now giving up to the torpor induced by the waters of the lethal fountain, they sank in each other's arms down upon a blossom-embroidered hillock. Here the following day the glories of the early morning sun found the lovers thus at length, dead amidst the great flowering trees.

And here an archroyal searching-party finally discovered their bodies, already beautiful with dis-solution, some thirty days later. Noting their nearness to the dread Fountain of Ddath, the officials comprehended at once the sad issue within that place. And thus did the end come upon the lovers Lailis and Ampara, and poets everywhere sang of their love and of their sad conclusion, and the Archking himself, among many, mourned their passing.

THE SHEPHERD AND THE SHEPHERDESS

Now here we have a pretty tale of a shepherd and a shepherdess, Laillquis and Xilvaä . . . this happened in the sixth century of the third milennium of the Atlantean Empire. And it came to pass that of the seven sons fathered by Atlas CXXIX, or Atlas Lissarion, the youngest one, to wit, the Prince Atlantaon, once again wearied of the perennial splendor, the everlasting pomp and pageantry, of the imperial court and capital. Aon, as his close friends and relatives would sometimes call him, decided to leave Atlantis the City for awhile, and to become a shepherd once again but this time somewhere in the eastern range of the Eiphlox Mountains which dominate and cradle the great mountain-heart-land Poseidonis. In addition, and of far greater import, the time had come for Aon to find himself a wife, according to that immemorial custom which dictates that the males of the upper classes must—almost always—choose their spouses from the lower classes.

With his dark-blond hair and his sea-green eyes, and with his unpretentious and practical garments of simple design and weave, Aon made a very pretty shepherd indeed. Leaving the imperial seat, he journeyed afoot north through the Great Vale of Atlantis, and then northeast into the eastern Eiphlox Mountains. On a warm and vernal day he wandered into the high mountain-village of Quolyx, a sheepherding community, close to two large sylvan lakes that lay just to the north like two huge light-blue eyes eternally gazing at the sky. Now the villagers did mark the great comeliness of the stranger who, holding converse with some elders in the village square, let it be known that he, Laillquis, an itinerant shepherd, was looking for work. And the elders, pointing to a large cot standing on the northern side of the square, advised the stranger to ask of old Septemmis, the wealthiest shepherd in the village.

Now Septemmis had just lost the shepherd of his flocks pastured at the western end of the western lake. After questioning the applicant closely, the squire pronounced himself satisfied, and instructed Lailliquis to claim charge of the flocks that very day. The newly-hired shepherd assented but as he was leaving the house of Septemmis he noticed a girl with dark-blue eyes and raven-black hair . . . a girl of wondrous beauty and gracious bearing and enigmatical presence whom the squire introduced as his daughter Xilvaä. And the maiden and the youth . . . each intrigued and enchanted the other. . . .

Every day Xilvaä came to visit the handsome stranger who told her of the great world that lay beyond the little village; and he charmed her with stories of the great imperial court and capital that flourish in everlasting splendor close to the Ocean Sea. Deeply but gradually the youth and the maiden fell in love with each other. After careful deliberation, the lovers decided to ask permission for their union from Xilvaä's father.

Septemmis not only refused, explaining that he had hopes of a high-placed husband for his daughter, but reprimanded Lailliquis and instructed him to return to his flocks. Also, wishing to keep the lovers apart, the old shepherd banished his daughter to the eastern end of the eastern lake, to tend his flocks thereat.

Greatly did the lovers grieve at being parted, and every morning and every evening they both wept into the opposite ends of their respective lakes. Anon a strange phenomenon occurred: the western lake slowly changed its wonted light-blue color to a lovely sea-green, like that in the eyes of the shepherd Lailliquis; and the eastern lake slowly changed its wonted light-blue color to a rich azurine, like that in the eyes of the sphepherdess Xilvaä; and the waters in the passage connecting the two lakes turned to an aquamarine.

Now all the villagers did mark this weird occurrence, and many of them spoke sternly with Septemmis, advising him that surely he did an evil thing, thus to part two lovers whose love had proven so great that their tears of grief at being parted could alter the color of two large bodies of water. But Septemmis would not be moved, maintaining that the weird change of color was purely coincidental, and had resulted without a doubt from some natural cause.

Lailliquis got word of his plight to his father, and anon the Archking with great pomp and with a great entourage sought the solace of the high mountain-country in and around Quolyx, ostensibly to hunt. Great was the joy of them that dwelt in the village at having their living deity in their midst, and great was their delight to see the grand pavilions of the archroyal encampment, gay with rich and brilliant colors, rising up like bright enormous flowers in the glades and on the hillocks environing the village. Privately Atlas Lissarion spoke with Aon, advising him not to grieve: he, the Archking, would intercede with Septemmis.

Summoning the old shepherd, the Archking told him that he had heard that Septemmis dreamt of a high-placed husband for his daughter. The old man, amazed at the Archking's private knowledge, became confused and uncertain, but assented to the fact. Then Lissarion inquired closely of the old man whether he would oppose a match between Xilvaä and the Archking's own youngest son, to wit, the Prince Atlantaon. In even greater amazement the old man stated not only an emphatic nay but also that he could only regard such a match as the greatest he could possibly *imagine* for Xilvaä.

Then the Archking inquired more closely, "But why do you then oppose this match in fact, even though you say that you would not? For is not Atlantaon, sometimes called Aon, sometimes called *Lailliquis,* my very own son, who presently grieves, as does indeed your very own daughter, that you should separate them? And has not their weeping, as a very proof of their great love, changed the color of the twin lakes hereby? Do you still refuse to be moved now?"

And now the amazement and the wonder of Septemmis grew to their greatest; and covered with confusion immingled with some shame, the old man sheepishly but gladly gave his official approval to the union of the shepherd called Lailliquis and of the shepherdess called Xilvaä.

RECIPROCITY

This is a tale that Pharanos, the present astrologer to the Archking, loves to tell about his former astrological magister, to wit, Ullfanon. Ullfanon, it will be recalled, served as Astrologer Archroyal—and hence as Prince of Astrologers in All the Empire of Atlantis—first of all to Atlas CLII, or Atlas Quomequa, and then to his widow, the former Queen Consort Archroyal, and the first and only queen regnant in all the history of Atlantis, the Great Queen Archroyal, to wit, Atlaïs Atalantossa. Once a year, usually after the autumnal aequinox, and always at night, during a time whenas neither clouds nor mist nor fog would obscure the heavens, Ullfanon was wont to sit in full astrological robes and regalia upon the great astrological throne that centrally stands within the central and highest edifice of the archroyal observatory rising from the highest heights of Mount Atlantis.

Thus would Ullfanon hold solitary court from the dusk of evening until the dusk of morning, virtually unmoving, wrapped in meditation, and listening to the music of the spheres. Above him would loom his largest heaven-sweeping telescope, but with the thick cylinder of the telescope completely reversed, and thus with the eye-piece proffered as it were for the possible use of anyone or anything out in sidereal space, anyone or anything that might care to look down and inspect the old astrologer. Then, on that one unique night, he would ceremoniously invite the stars, the very stars and suns themselves, to study him, Ullfanon, as he had studied them, the stars, on all the other nights whenas the local meteorological conditions permitted such scrutiny and contemplation. Thus did Ullfanon allow the stars, if so they deigned, to give him something equivalent to that scrutiny and love that he proffered them in his eye and in his heart eternally.

This tale I have on the best confidence from the present astrologer to the Archking, to wit, Pharanos, who (it will be recalled) studied with Ullfanon as his last pupil and apprentice.

THE IFFINNIX

The poets and the prophets, those masters of strange lore and knowledge, assert that somewhere high in the highest mountains of the great central range of the Eiphlox Mountains, and thus north of the Outhanox, the Great Citadel of Poseidonis, there abides—according to the most reliable traditions—the now near-legendary bird called the iffinnix, who can fly to greater heights than any other wingèd creature, although the peaks of the greatest Eiphlox Mountains rise up even beyond the reach of the iffinnix.

They say that now but one last iffinnix lives on, a miracle of avian loveliness, with pinions of murex and gold and flame, and that all the others of his kind have long since departed for other worlds, but that he, the very last one, cannot leave our sphere until the eventual foundering of Atlantis, that will come about sometime during these latter cycles.

And both the poets and the prophets predict that when the very last iffinnix leaves Atlantis, when Atlantis has thus verily come to know an empire of many waters, then and then only shall he sing at last his only song, ineffable and canorous and poignant like the musical note of swans before their death.

A VISION OF STRANGE SPLENDOR

1. I dreamed a dream: a million-colored rose unfolded to my view. Standing on an empty plain beneath an empty sky, I watched both the plain and the sky gradually disappear, and I myself became concentred only to one enormous eye that could see in any direction, an eye that also had the power somehow to apprehend sound, an essence of audient vision somehow suspended in pure space. But somehow I knew that I lay at the bottom of some innominate abyss.

2. Of a sudden a great mass of ever-seething flame and smoke uprose, seemingly from nowhere. With sonorities as of a million thunders, the great mass of smoke and flame, firmly fixed upon the nothingness of the nadir, uncoiled swiftly to the zenith, with lights upon lights upon lights of a strange, septuple splendor.

3. Anon a weird, half-veiled illuminescence hovered over and out from this outré phenomenon, and suddenly at the top of the great mass of smoke and flame, a rosebud appeared, a rosebud curiously black and white and gray, a rosebud which waxed fuller and fuller, suddenly to burst forth in riotous bloom incredible, with a million petals and with a million colors, filling space as far as the eye could see.

4. Now this million-colored rose began to expand further and further, again filling space as far as the eye could see. And anon, deep within the profounds of the million-colored petals, I perceived tiny particles of incandescent matter which I suddenly recognized as innumerable stars around which there circled in unending cycles other stars as well as moons and planets.

5. Now all these atoms or stars began to circle around the great central eye which, I belatedly noticed, could perceive in all directions at once. Over and over, the atoms or stars wheeled around the great central eye in a deliberate and pre-measured music that seemed to have no end and no beginning. And now the splendors of that far-flung rose waxed ever brighter, with colors and lights never imagined and never to be imagined.

6. And once again the million-colored rose began to expand further

and further, again filling space as far as the eye could see. And somehow I knew that the million-colored rose had reached her uttermost growth, her uttermost bloom. What an infinity of atoms and stars nestled in her petals! In that one great expansive jet of light . . . a resplendent fountainhead or matrix of innumerable and innominate shapes and forms and fantasies . . . I perceived and understood the essential unity of everyone and everything.

7. Anon the stars or atoms grew faint and began to fail, and the million-colored rose began to withdraw back upon and into herself. Then with a suddenness unexpected as it was frightening, the rose burst into great and all-consuming flame. But through the flames I was able still to perceive a rosebud of pristine beauty, a rosebud curiously black and white and gray. The rosebud vanished and in her place a fiery alpha appeared, endued with incredible splendors. Anon the multi-colored splendors of the alpha changed to a single phosphorescent and compassionate blue, and then the alpha disappeared. And then I and the eye and the vision became one. And then I woke.

And here concludes
the little book yclept
the Minor Chronicles
of Atlantis.

KILCOLMAN CASTLE: 20 AUGUST 1965

(In the fellow-ship of Kirby McCauley.)

"Yet all these were, when no man did them know;
Yet have from wisest ages hidden been:
And later times things more unknown shall show.
Why then should witless man so much misween
That nothing is, but that which he hath seen?
What if within the Moon's fair shining sphere?
What if in every other star unseen,
Of other worlds he happily should hear?
He wonder would much more: yet such to some appear."
                    Edmund Spenser, *The Faerie Queene,* II: Proem: III.

Here, where the wind, the rain, the muted sun combine
To form the glistening dream of this cool summer's day,
To this place have we come as pilgrims to your shrine:—
Here, where these hills, these fields, this little lake still stay;
Where, arrased on this tower, the ivy's rich display
Of deep green still keeps green the bay-leaves in your crown:
The one white swan upon the lake in some strange way,
However brief, renews far better your renown
Than monuments which man puts up . . . which time and man bring
      down. . . .

Now soon, as you yourself presage, the knights of Earth shall wend
Upon their quest, their destined quest, with all the stars for crown,
Into the hypercosmic Vast sublime and without end. . . .
Then, to the sound of otherworldly harp and flute and horn,
The phoenix heart and soul of man shall once more be reborn.

AUBADE

Translated from the Atlantean of Prince Atlantarion.

" . . . The choir, / Ere dawn, of little birds. . . ."

The early morning dew lies over all—
The garden-close, the field, the woods, the glade—
Now, ere the dusk yields up her pearl-gray pall:
Restless, alert, the little birds invade
This tapestry of pallid light and shade,
And fill the air with many a joyful cry:
While yet the birds attend with serenade,
Out of the east where never sunsets die,
The sun's fierce disk of pale flame-gold climbs up the sky.

GREEN SLEEVES
(1967)

Upon hearing the Fantasia on "Greensleeves"
by Ralph Vaughan Williams.

Forth from the heart of hill and field and hearth;
Of castle, palace, manor house and cot;
Of lush-green park and woods and garden-garth;—
This tune, quick with the beat of life and fraught
With long-dead voices otherwise forgot,
Still sings today with slow, deliberate breath;—
This melody that centuries have wrought;
Born long before the first Elizabeth
Out of Old England's earth, but past all earthly death:

Elizabeth the Second reigns throughout these years—
Today—so that this twice-old air gains now new breath,
To mingle with the music of the far-off spheres. . . .

This tune, the breath of lush-green park and woods and garden-garth,
Forever sings forth from the heart of hill and field and hearth.

O BEAUTIFUL DARK-AMBER EYES OF OLD

Translated from the French of Michel de Labretagne.

O beautiful dark-amber eyes of old:
Did I not know them in the long ago?
Within a boscage deep and manifold,
Again I am the unicorn . . . and, lo!
You are the maid, the cause of all my woe,
Dressed in a gown of sendaline and gold,
To whom in gentle trust and love I go,
To lay my horn upon your lap. . . . Behold!
These beautiful dark-amber eyes I know from old.

THE FORSAKEN PALACE

Dedicated to Algernon Charles Swinburne, in memoriam.

> "In the world of dreams I have chosen my part,
>   To sleep for a season and hear no word
> Of true love's truth or of light love's art,
>   Only the song of a secret bird."
>   Swinburne, *A Ballad of Dreamland,* Envoy.

An endless maze of colonnades, it lies
In a vast woods to-north, yet always green,
Beneath eternally mist-haunted skies:
Within the countless courts that lie between
The colonnades, full in the pallid sheen
Of sun or moon, great fountains roar and gush:
Telling of legends tragic or serene,
Vague-figured tapestries of purple plush
Hang in the gloom of halls and chambers all ahush. . . .

Where dawn-red roses bloom deep in the innermost court,
A golden bird, within whose plumes wild splendors flush,
Sings yet a sea-like song, and holds his lonely court:

With notes and chords and overtones that endlessly prolong,
Not far away to west, the sea forever sings her song.

FOR THE "SHAPES OF CLAY" OF AMBROSE BIERCE

Lo! vague, inchoate shapes of clay that stand
Alone upon a bleak and moonlit sweep
Of desert barren save of night-black sand:
Lo! in their midst, huge marble gods that keep
Close watch upon those shapes of clay, and weep
Forth tears of ebon amber all around:
Lo! high above, deep in the cosmic deep,
A vast and kaolin moon whose rays astound
That land of spellbound sight forever to no sound.

CONNAISSANCE FATALE

Where gnarled gnomes and where haggard hags convene
In some huge sepulchre deep in the earth;
There, where the lovely lamia reigns as queen
Amid Walpurgis revelry and mirth;
There, where the basilisk gives loathsome birth
To monstrous brood; there, there I met my love,
That Atlantean solace for all dearth,
That primal goddess from domains above,—
Fair Lilith,—she wherein unite the serpent and the dove:

We kissed but once—but once!—eternity of heaven and hell—
And then she vanished instantly: And now what other love
Could give me her warm lips of mandragore and asphodel?

For me, no place to rest, no time for love, no end of pain,
Until sometime, somehow, somewhere, I claim her lips again.

FOR THE "BLACK BEETLES IN AMBER" OF AMBROSE BIERCE

Night-black heraldic scarabaeuses
Painstakingly carven by a master hand
Out of the blackest of black onyxes:
Then through the black arts of an elder land
Set in a cartouche of golden amber and,
At last, ensepulchred within the earth:
Then aeons later from the amber sand
Reborn, in blackly splendor-fraught rebirth,
Thus to attest the Night, and Her eternal worth.

OFFRANDE EXOTIQUE

Dedicated to Eulalie, in memoriam.

" 'Tis a sweet theme,
Which many a muse before has tried;—
   Let none now deem
The hands profane which touch the lyre;
They but essay (it were no crime t'aspire)
To sing again that oft-sung tale:
The May-Rose and the Nightingale!"
                              Eulalie, *Approach of May.*

These little buds, these blossoms, and these leaves,
I proffer but in vain: For who shall take
These now? or sun-proud fruit? or gold-green sheaves
Of grain? or sunlight on a sylvan lake?
Or foam that flowers forth within the wake
Of some great quinquireme ablaze with light?
Or all such things that make the spirit ache
And thrill with yet an ever-new delight?—
But manifold are those who take these blooms that grow by night:

Mandragoras in pale or purple avatars,
Huge calla lilies of a pure but deathly white,
Black roses, and black poppies, and black nenuphars:

Take then these coronals of blossoms dark or wan,
And seek no more those blooms that have forever gone.

SONNETS ON AN EMPIRE OF MANY WATERS

Dedicated to Kirby McCauley.

LEGEND

The Empire of Atlantis

1. Atlantis (at-LAN-tiss), the Archkingdom:
   the Mid-Atlantic Ridge and the Azores.
2. Gades (guh-DEEZ): a projection of land
   off southwest Iberia.

3. Atlantigades (AT-lan-TIG-uh-deez):
   the Madeira Islands.
4. Atkantharia (AT-kan-THARR-ee-uh):
   the Canary Islands.

5. Iffrikonn-Yssthia (IFF-rih-konn, ISS-thee-uh):
   the Cape Verde Islands.
6. Atalantessys (AT-uh-lan-TESS-iss):
   the St. Peter and St. Paul Rocks.

7. Atlantillia (AT-lan-TILL-ee-uh): island
   between Greater Antilles and Lesser Antilles.
8. Atatemthessys (AT-uh-TEM-theh-siss):
   the Bermuda Islands.

9. At-Thulonn (AT-thu-LONN): island
   off southeast Greenland.
10. Avalonessys (AV-uh-law-NESS-iss):
    island in the Irish Sea.

11. Poseidonis (PO-see-DONN-iss),
    the Archprincedom:
    the mountain-heart-land
    of the Archkingdom:
    the Azores.

SONNETS ON AN EMPIRE OF MANY WATERS

I

Here, where the fountains of the deep-sea flow
In fair resemblance of eternity,
And where the lights of deep-sea creatures glow
But faintly in the black infinity;
There stand vague shapes of huge antiquity—
Colossal fanes, and vasty palaces,
And markets once alive with merchantry,
And obelisks, like monstrous phalluses,
Outline the streets of this deep-sea metropolis:

And where proud kings and princes pomped in splendor near-divine,
Within the Great Thronehall Archroyal, within the Acropolis;
The tentacles of giant squids in darkness now entwine. . . .

Yea, even as foretold by mystic prophets long ago,
A boundless ocean-empire hath Atlantis come to know.

SONNETS ON AN EMPIRE OF MANY WATERS

II

ATLANTIS

Translated from the Atlantean of Athallarion.

With land's ends three, southeast, southwest, and north—
An alpha huge athwart a great blue shield—
This mighty island kingdom stretches forth:
From inland mountain and from inland weald
To where the ocean's many waters yield
To coastal mountain, tableland, and vale:
From upland forest and from upland field
To where the sea-grove stretches from the gale;
To fiords, to bays, to gulfs where sports the migrant whale:

And in the southern midst, circled by mountains and by hills,—
The Great Vale of Atlantis,—where the harvests never fail,
But always yield rich gold of grains for Atlantean mills. . . .

Behold how this almighty island kingdom stretches forth:
One, to the southeast; two, to the southwest; three, to the north!

SONNETS ON AN EMPIRE OF MANY WATERS

III

GADES

Translated from the Atlantean of Athallarion.

Land of the taurus and the taurokamp,
Keeper of the Gates to the Seas Within,
And of the eastern realms the guardian-lamp:
In puissance and in wealth the closest kin
Unto Atlantis—Lo! her royal twin—
This is the port for ships from every part
Of the lands that front on the Seas Within . . .
Vessels that bring their goods, their works of art,
From many a mart nearby, from many a far-off mart. . . .

Here, at the brave sunsetting, with strange reverence and rite,
Out of his steaming chest, nude youths wrench forth the great bull's
     heart,
To read therein deep omens, ere the imminence of night:

Yes, of the Empire's eastern realms the guardian and the lamp,
This is the strong domain of the taurus and the taurokamp.

SONNETS ON AN EMPIRE OF MANY WATERS

IV

ATLANTIGADES

Translated from the Atlantean of Athallarion.

This kingdom of the Yndessessian vine,
The green, the purple, and the yellow grape,
The opulent and multi-varied wine;
Regally spreads out upon her three-pronged shape,
West, east, and south—from mountaintop to cape—
Her lush-green vineyard-forest without end;
None of whose ripe grape-clusters can escape
The keen, sure eye of harvesters who wend
Throughout those wilding labyrinths wherein the berries pend:

Give me to drink of your good wine, your vintage made for kings—
Quintessence wherewithin the earth, the rain, the sunlight blend—
Till I, like Majesty, shall muse on thrice-resplendent things:

Between Atlantis and Gades, replete with grapes and wine,
There stands up out of the ocean's deeps this grand realm of the vine.

SONNETS ON AN EMPIRE OF MANY WATERS

V

ATKANTHARIA

Translated from the Atlantean of Athallarion.

Upon the huge crescent of this arid isle,
These irrigated pomegranate-trees
Thrive in unending orchards, mile on mile:
Like images depicted in a frieze,
They scarcely move within the ghostly breeze
Breathing from off the sea-foam all in bloom:
Thrust up above the rows on rows of trees,
The stark and snow-topped mountains loom and loom,
Yet fires from eld still flow throughout their deep-set womb:

And fires from eld still burn deep in the garnets of these pomes,
Still flame deep in these flowers, these bright-red stars without perfume,
Still illuminate these leaves where yet some primordial splendor homes:

These irrigated pomegranate-trees, for mile on mile,
Flower, leaf, and fruit . . . upon the huge crescent of this arid isle.

SONNETS ON AN EMPIRE OF MANY WATERS

VI

IFFRIKONN-YSSTHIA

Translated from the Atlantean of Athallarion.

Above the tropic seas' dark azurine
Which mirrors back the sky's unbroken dome,
There rises up this labyrinth of green:
Below these proud and snow-crowned peaks there roam
Those cats that have within these woods their home,
Tiger and panther, lion and spotted pard:
Fantastic orchids white as arctic foam,
Against the deep and mothering jungle starred,
Blossom above the night-black shores which granite headlands guard:

In answer to the roaring breakers out beyond the lee,—
From deep within those glooms with twisting vines and branches
    barred
The great bull elephant roars out his challenge at the sea:

With tall proud peaks, this jungle-isle, a labyrinth of green,
Looms up above the tropic seas and their dark azurine.

SONNETS ON AN EMPIRE OF MANY WATERS

VII

ATALANTESSYS

Translated from the Atlantean of Athallarion.

Far southern kingdom of gigantic flowers,
And marble palaces upon the shore,
Or in the midst of gardens, groves, and bowers:
Great golden poppies in the sunlight pour
Forth auras like a dust of golden ore—
Huge orchids in the shade bloom ebon-hued:
While grossly grow the flowers called mandragore,
Deep nenuphars, with tropical suns endued,
Spread out on pool and stream their own tremendous magnitude:

Borne on cold ocean-streams from ultimate antarctic bournes,
Masses of ice, like ships arch-fantasy-wise carved and hued,
Sail up offshore to melt away . . . whose passing no one mourns:

White palaces upon the shore, in gardens, groves, and bowers. . . .
Out of far southern seas there lifts the realm of gigantic flowers.

SONNETS ON AN EMPIRE OF MANY WATERS

VIII

ATLANTILLIA

Translated from the Atlantean of Athallarion.

This island kingdom of the jaguär,
 The orange, and the lemon, and the lime,
Is but the gate to realms more strange and far:
Like some fair visne surviving from Earth's prime,
With green growth never breathed upon by rime,
Between the twin Antillias lies this land:
 But far more fair than any wordly clime
 Is what the sunset and the clouds command,
Now, to the west, eternally beyond that further strand. . . .

And yet this island realm were paradise enough . . . for *here*
Can I not grasp these green, gamboge, and golden fruits in hand,
Can I not breathe the citrus flowers perfuming *everywhere*? . . .

This paradise enough, the gate to realms more strange and far,
Remains the green and regal isle where homes the jaguär.

SONNETS ON AN EMPIRE OF MANY WATERS

IX

ATATEMTHESSYS

Translated from the Atlantean of Athallarion.

Within this round the giant squid resides,
This wide round of volcanoes sub-marine,
And in the midst thereof this isle abides:
Superbious, majestical, serene,
The archimperial peacocks pomp and preen
Amid this paradise of flowering trees:
Both flowers and fruits peculiar to this visne,
Together with attendant courts of bees,
Hang out over the flood and ebb of semi-tropic seas:

Enthroned amid the water's many mansions and domains,
A great pulsating brain . . . encircled with arch-mysteries,
Far down below the giant squid in strange effulgence reigns:

Beyond the rise and fall of elder worlds, this isle abides
Within this mantic round wherein the giant squid resides.

SONNETS ON AN EMPIRE OF MANY WATERS

X

AT-THULONN

Translated from the Atlantean of Athallarion.

Far northern kingdom of the northern lights,
Of ice and snow and evergreen and frost,
Of endless twilights and of sunlit nights:—
Where winter winds work miracles embossed
With evanescent lights the skies have lost,
Preparing countless fantasies for view:—
Where lovely lads and maidens may accost
The unicorn, entrapping him; but few
Hunt other than the seal, the musk ox, or the caribou:

In autumn and in spring the northern lights unfurl,
With ever-changing veils of purple, green, and blue;
Orange, and red, and gold; and silver shot with pearl:

Endowed with ice and snow, with unending dusk and sunlit nights,
Southeast off Mhu Thulan there lies the land of strange north lights.

SONNETS ON AN EMPIRE OF MANY WATERS

XI

AVALONESSYS

Translated from the Atlantean of Athallarion.

Island of apples and of apple-wine,
Where rich and year-round crops of apples grow,
And apple-blossoms bloom above the brine!
You grant fair haven to the ships that go
Upon the Shoaling Seas' green crystalline flow—
Fair haven, with great harbors, and green coves:
Refuge and rest you grant; soft sea-winds blow
Adown your arbors where the sea-bird roves;
And lovers love to loiter deep within your groves. . . .

Pausing upon their northern or their southern flight,
To take a brief refreshment of your water-troves,
Amid your fragrant isle the great wild swans alight:

Island where apple-blossoms bloom above the brine. . . .
O realm divine with apples and with apple-wine!

SONNETS ON AN EMPIRE OF MANY WATERS

XII

POSEIDONIS

Translated from the Atlantean of Athallarion.

Cradle of empire and of mighty kings;
Great mountain-heart-land whose great mountains rise
Up far beyond the reach of any wings!
Tremendous bulks ascending to the skies
Beyond the heights whereto the phoenix flies,
Hereat they stand like puissant kings of old:
Upon their robes of evergreen there lies,
In lavish wise, the sunlight's breath of gold,
And fires their silver crowns with splendors white and cold:

Poseidonis, within the matrix of your Citadel,
The endless halls and corridors in funeral pomp enfold
Over three thousand kings and queens who thus for aye shall dwell:

Lo! these great peaks which rise beyond the reach of any wings,
Cradle this cradle-realm of empire and of mighty kings.

SONNETS ON AN EMPIRE OF MANY WATERS

XIII

THE MERCHANT-PRINCES

Translated from the Atlantean of Athallarion.

Outside the Great Gate Acropolitan,
Due south of Mount Atlantis, they await
In splendor more than necropolitan:
Their crowns and great rich robes all aureate,
The morning's white-gold rays irradiate
With lusters and with lights ineffable:
And shall he still come forth? The hour is late.
The tremors of suspense they cannot quell,
Nor yet the love and awe that in their hearts foretell. . . .

Now fanfares and alarums. . . . Soon shall he, the King, come forth,—
Empanoplied with archimperial splendors nonpareil. . . .
The merchant-princes have all faced the Gate upon the north:

In splendor more than that of those in some necropolis,
They wait within the Plaza south of the arch Acropolis.

SONNETS ON AN EMPIRE OF MANY WATERS

XIV

AN ARGOSY OF TRADE

Translated from the Atlantean of Athallarion.

Like some strange beast arisen from deep caves,
With triple banks of oars on either side,
Westward the barque pavanes across the waves:
The sign and sigil of an imperial pride,
A crown and trident spreads against the wide
And bleached-white sail its woven silhouette:
No land nor other ship may be descried
Here where dark seas and empty skies are met . . .
Where soon in fierce flame-gold the sun shall sink, and set:

A vast rich hoard the trireme holds within her cargo-glooms . . .
Furs from the north, wines from the south, lanterns and lamps of jet;
Argent, and or, and rare gem-stones, and opulent perfumes:

Westward an argosy of trade pavanes across the waves,
Like some strange beast with many legs arisen from deep caves.

SONNETS ON AN EMPIRE OF MANY WATERS

XV

MEMORIES OF THE ASTAZHAN

Translated from the Atlantean of Aänsess.

Beyond this tapestry of mist and rain
Which winter weaves about these northern hills,
Fair southern realms in memory still remain:
The Astazhan with all her splendor fills
This heart of me—her springs, and streams, and rills;
Her pools, her lakes; her pastures—lush and green —
On plains, in valleys, and on rolling hills;
Her parks, her woods; the warm but gentle sheen
Of the sun swathed with mist above her large demesne. . . .

Between the cots and castles graze the cows and goats and sheep,
While herdsmen, decked against a grass well-near aquamarine,
Still play upon rude pipes their song of peace and rest and sleep:

Here, in the north, fair southern realms in memory still remain
Beyond this tapestry which winter weaves of mist and rain.

SONNETS ON AN EMPIRE OF MANY WATERS

XVI

A LETTER FROM VALOTH

Translated from the Atlantean of Aänsess.

From Aänsess, Archknight, Archroyal Governor of the Atlantean Forts and Watchtowers in Valoth, Karanak, and southern Ivvrinaä; to His Majesty, King Atlantarion I, Overlord of the Empire of Atlantis; Dictated from Apenderragon the Great Watchtower in southern Valoth but Three Days after the Great Catacylsm.

My prince, our Avalonessys is now no more:
Upon that single day and night of rain,
Beyond the reckoning of the utmost shore,
With all earth shuddering as in fear and pain,
Slowly the island sank below the main,
Leaving behind a foam-filled wrath unknown,
More bleak and barren than an arctic plain,
A desolation utterless and lone,
Where winds and waves now mourn, and make imperial moan:

The blossoms of the foam, a white and fatal green,
Now bloom above those miles of apple-blossoms flown
Beneath a deeper sea no longer fair and green:

Submerged beyond the reckoning of the utmost shore,
Alas, my prince, our Avalonessys is now no more!

SONNETS ON AN EMPIRE OF MANY WATERS

XVII

No, not until the final age of Earth,
When man has gone, and nothing claims the land,
Shall this proud city know a new rebirth:
The sea shall dwindle to its utmost strand;
The deep-sea silt shall change to fine gray sand,
Then like a vasty pall shall fall away:
And then Atlantis once again shall stand
Resplendent in the splendidness of day;
Until—at last—her last, and very last, decay...

When all her fair proud ruin shall dissolve to dust,
And thus, to dust dissolved, forevermore shall stay;
For *in* the end, unjust or just, the end *is* just:

For in the end the Earth itself shall surely not outlast,—
Less than a speck of cosmic dust slow-dwindling on the Vast. . . .

FINIS

TO AN ATLANTEAN POET

For D. S. F.

Dear friend, you walk alone in Atlantean fields,
So long enshrouded by the water's swell,
Where coral-encrusted palaces beneath the waves
Dream in sea change the dreams no man can tell
Save you who sing of lovers long rememberèd,
Of older glories in a shining world,
Of banners, pageants, distant sea-drenched drums
Vibrating in the waters:
Then once more there comes
The lord of sea and land,
And by his side,
Iridescent his bride,
And the older loves that are rememberèd.

Glory fades, dreams die.
We live in the gray land.
Touch for a moment my hand.
We remember the king and his immemorial queen.
                                    MARGO SKINNER.

San Francisco, California.
11 August 1967.

(By permission of Margo Skinner.)

INSPIRATION

Dedicated in sincere friendship to D. S. F.

Bared branches wave leafless fronds
    Aloft, and my eyes ascend
Yet further and above
To limpid folds of blue and flakèd white
Wherein the portraits of the Gods
    Find place in fitful majesty
Commanding the minds of men
    To behold Omnipotence. . . .
In spheres of sapphirine splendour.

From beyond, in rich Atlantean climes
    Across those lulling waters,
I hear swelling chorus mass
    Upon swelling chorus
Billowing forth into One
    Eternal Note
Sustaining Universes
    In its wake
And of its substance I partake
    As with each and all.

                     IAN M. LAW.

Beckenham, Kent, England.
9 December 1967.

    (By permission of Ian M. Law.)

SECRETEST

To Donald Fryer,
upon his nearing completion
of Songs and Sonnets Atlantean.

Andromeda and Messier Twenty-Five;
Black shadows of the planets and the moons;
Unseen electric rays, vocal and terse;
Caverns within Altair and Deneb Two;
From mists 'round Procyon, a priceless dew;
The deepest secrets of the universe!
And beauty's sweep in Mars's red sand dunes—
Dry, baked by gamma rays, and still alive!

The bathysphere falls down the ebon height,
Bearing adventurers extramarine;
Ooze, and the pillowed stop; the searchlight's beam
Shows great Atlantis standing still supreme—
Might of the depths!—and so much to be seen.
Just so, through modern glooms, Fryer shines bright.

FRITZ LEIBER.

Composed on PSA flight 722,
San Francisco to Los Angeles,
22 June 1969.

(By permission of Fritz Leiber.)

TO GLORIA KATHLEEN

For my very own Queen Gloriana.

My lover-lass, my lady fair, my friend,
You are the sole illusion worth my while
This moment just before the cycles end:
Our love creates an Atlantean isle
Where hell with paradise must reconcile,
And heaven and hell subsume the masque of pain:
For still, within our kiss, within our smile,
Inheres the still small point beyond all bane,
Inheres the loss of self and, thus, the loss of all things vain. . . .

The vanities that fret shall fall from us, and all things chime
In chords tremendous, deep, sublime . . . that endlessly wax and wane
To pulsings of that one pure fire beyond all space or time:

The sole illusion worth my while before the cycles end,
You throne supreme . . . my lover-lass, my lady fair, my friend.

DONALD S. FRYER.

San Francisco, California.
Christmas 1969.

FOR MASTER EDMUND SPENSER HIS GREAT SONG

Two stanzas for The Faerie Queene.

VII: Proem: I.

You ask, Who *is* this famous Faerie Queene,
Whom we so much do praise, yet nowhere show,
But always vouch, although but seldom seen?
Mistress of shapes and changes whom we know,
Transcendent, immanent, both weal and woe,
The source of all things noble, just, serene;
This sovereign lady fair from long ago,
This presence often felt, yet seldom seen,
Lo! Sapience or Mother Nature *is* our Faerie Queene.

VII: VIII: III.

But since that Sabaoths sight may never be
Whilst here on Earth we needs must wend our way
And suffer changeful state, then list grant me,
O that great Sabbaoth God, the strength to play
My bardic lute, and sing my wonted lay,
My song of wars and loves which will not cease
Until the reckoning of that seventh day
Whenas all things from change will find release,
To rest back in their source, that still small point called peace.

MASTER DONALD SIDNEY-FRYER.

San Francisco, California.
30 September 1970.

NOTES

by Dr. Ibid M. Andor

NOTES, by Dr. Ibid M. Andor.

To an Atlantean Poet, by Margo Skinner; *Inspiration,* by Ian M. Law; *Secretest,* by Fritz Leiber; *To Gloria Kathleen,* by Donald S. Fryer; and *For Master Edmund Spenser His Great Song,* by Master Donald Sidney-Fryer.

These six poems are included here in the same way as commendatory verses by friends and well-wishers, as well as dedicatory verses by the poet himself, were included in collections of Elizabethan poetry, thus to invoke a favorable ambiance for the author and his book. The title "The Lord of Sea and Land" (see line 10 of Margo Skinner's poem *To an Atlantean Poet*) was one of the official designations of each of the ten Atlantean kings.

Dedicated, in this the reign of Elizabeth II, to the memory of Edmund Spenser, poet laureate to Elizabeth I.

Since most of the poems in verse included in this book are cast in some form of the Spenserian sonnet and/or Spenserian stanza, the entire volume constitutes in effect an extended act of homage to "England's Arch-poët"—to wit, Edmund Spenser—hence, the dedication.

The Spenserian stanza-sonnet by "G. W. Senior, to the Author" forms (that is, in terms of what has reached us from the Age of Elizabeth I) the most pointed anticipation of the form devised or innovated by Mr. Fryer from Spenser's own sonnet-form as well as from his own stanza. Line 1: "Colin" or "Colin Clout" is of course Spenser himself. Lines 1-2: A reference to Spenser beginning his career "in lowly

vein" with the twelve "aeglogues" that make up *The Shepheardes Calender,* first published in 1579. Lines 3-4: A reference to *The Faerie Queene.* Lines 5-6: A reference to the *Amoretti and Epithalamion.* Lines 13-14: The recent restoration of Spenser to his place of pre-eminence in English letters, by the outstanding Spenserian scholars of the 1960's, thoroughly vindicates the sentiment voiced with such confidence by "G. W. Senior" in these lines. Spenser proved indeed the "perfect guide" to the Elizabethan poets.

Introduction, by Dr. Ibid M. Andor.

Unless otherwise indicated, all quotations—used to identify the particular topic or point under discussion—derive from the *Introduction.*

Pronunciations for Atlantean proper names, etc. Atlantean: AT-lan-TEE-un. Atlantis: at-LAN-tiss. Poseidonis: PO-see-DONN-iss. Codex Atlanteanus: CO-dex AT-lahn-tay-AH-noose. Aänsess: AY-ahn-sess. Atlantarion: AT-lan-TARR-ee-un. Aïs: eye-EESS. Apenderragon: AH-pen-DARE-uh-gonn. Valoth: vuh-LOTH. Outhanox: OO-thuh-nox. Xonorr: k'zo-NORR. Astazhan: AH-stuh-ZHAHN.

For those readers who are interested in learning more about the history of the *Codex Atlanteanus,* as well as about its actual form and substance (as derived from the *Roman* by Labretagne, as well as from such of his comparatively few notes as are preserved in the Bibliothèque Nationale in Paris), the monograph by the present annotator entitled *The Codex Atlanteanus Reconstructed* (first published in 1936, and now in its 31st edition) will provide the most extensive and authoritative detail (The New England Institute of Oceanography Press, Provincetown, Cape Cod, Massachusetts).

Virtually all the Atlantean poetry surviving either through *La Jouvence Bretagnesque* or through the *Roman* by Labretagne, dates from the last hundred years or so *before* the Great Cataclysm or from the seven-and-thirty years *after* the Great Cataclysm, more or less.

"The Spenserian stanza itself, in terms of its actual use by poets, has declined steadily since around 1900, and finds virtually no employment at all today, oddly enough, in this the Neo-Elizabethan Age."

The use of an isolated Spenserian stanza as a vehicle for lyric expression, it may be mentioned here, is rare. The form has usually been used of course in long poems, as part of an over-all series of Spenserian stanzas. The great Irish fantaisiste, Lord Dunsany, was one of the few poets of the 20th century who would on occasion favor the Spenserian stanza as the basis for a single short lyric.

"The reader will note that the rime-scheme of the Spenserian stanza as well as that of the first nine lines of the Spenserian sonnet are thus exactly the same."

Neither Spenser nor his contemporaries were unaware of the over-all similarity between the Spenserian stanza and the Spenserian sonnet, or of a natural formal break that could occur between lines 9 and 10, and between lines 12 and 13, in the Spenserian sonnet. Spenser evidently evolved his particular sonnet-form just sometime previous to the publication of the first

three books of *The Faerie Queene* in 1590: the Spenserian sonnet-form made its official literary début in the 17 dedicatory sonnets included at the end of this first quarter of his magnum opus. It is most likely that the system of interlinking rimes in the stanza that he created for *The Faerie Queene* suggested to him a sonnet-form with a similar system of inter-linking rimes: from the A B A B B C B C C of the Spenserian stanza it is an easy and logical step to the A B A B B C B C C D C D E E of the Spenserian sonnet.

Spenser's contemporaries would have remarked the similarity between the stanza and the sonnet not only by the interlinking rime-scheme: just as the Spenserian stanza concludes regularly with an alexandrine, six of the 17 dedicatory Spenserian sonnets conclude regularly with an alexandrine; these are numbers 7, 9, 10, 14, 15, and 17.

In 1595 appeared the 89 sonnets included in Spenser's *Amoretti and Epithalamion,* and addressed for the most part to his second wife Elizabeth Boyle. All of the sonnets in this remarkable and beautiful sequence are Spenserian, with the exception of VIII which is Elizabethan, or Shakespearian, in form. Only two sonnets conclude with an alexandrine; these are numbers X and XLV.

But the second of the two commendatory sonnets (prefacing the *Amoretti*) by "G. W. Senior, to the Author"—the which appears on the dedication-page of the present volume —remains the most pointed anticipation of the Spenserian stanza-sonnet, and proves as much as any by Spenser himself to what extent both Spenser and his contemporaries were aware of the over-all similarity between the

Spenserian stanza and the Spenserian sonnet.

"The Spenserian stanza . . . consists of two quatrains and a final alexandrine (or, very rarely, a fourteener), all of which are linked by rime. . . ."

Few scholars appear to have commented on the fact that, whether line 9 of the Spenserian stanza is an alexandrine or a fourteener, or a sixteener for that matter, the effect is the same just so long as this last line succeeding eight decasyllabics is a line longer than the usual pentameter. There is only one official fourteener (by Spenser himself) ending a Spenserian stanza, out of the thousands of such stanzas that make up *The Faerie Queene*. This is at the end of stanza 42 in Canto XI of Book III, and runs as follows: "On whom he got faire Pegasus, that flitteth in the ayre." (This line refers to Neptune begetting the wingèd horse on "snaky-locke Medusa.") It may be mentioned here that both Shelley and Dr. Johnson have also written Spenserian stanzas ending with fourteeners.

Also, even if a Spenserian stanza is arranged in alexandrines (lines 1-8) and a fourteener or a sixteener (line 9) instead of being arranged in the usual decasyllabics and alexandrine; the effect again remains the same, just so long as the poet retains the over-all proportions; the principal difference being an increase in stateliness gained by the Spenserian stanza created in longer lines.

Likewise, few scholars appear to have commented on the formal advantage of the riming arguments that precede all the cantoes in *The Faerie Queene*. Each argument is cast in the old ballad metre (8: 6: 8: 6) or in the form of two fourteeners arranged in ballad metre (the effect of course remains the same), with the break or caesura usually falling nicely at the end of lines one and three, id est, at the end of the eighth syllable. These riming arguments not only inform the reader apropos of the substance of each canto; but metrically, in terms of a line longer than the wonted decasyllabic, they anticipate the stately beauty of the alexandrine that almost always closes each stanza, and oftentimes they possess the same alexandrine-like pendulum-effect.

"Another feature of the Spenserian stanza-sonnet which the reader will note in some of the poems assembled herein, is the rondeau-like device whereby line three more or less repeats as line thirteen (the first line of the final couplet), and line one more or less repeats as line fourteen (the second line of the final couplet); both lines usually lengthened, and hence both with appropriate additions and/or alterations."

The rondeau-like device could perhaps be called with greater propriety the rondel-device, and here we are thinking in particular—anent the effect of repetition—of the Swinburnian variation of the roundel, the English adaptation of the French rondel. This last form, the rondel, usually contains fourteen lines, of which the first two repeat as a refrain at lines 7 and 8, and again at lines 13 and 14. Compare this to the rondeau-like device whereby lines 1 and 3 more or less repeat as lines 14 and 13, respectively.

"Thus this volume has two principal purposes: to render into English the first considerable body of poems from the Atlantean, and to render direct homage to the *poet* (1552?-1599), and not the dramatist, whom the Elizabethans themselves held as supreme."

That the Elizabethans regarded Edmund Spenser as their supreme poet is demonstrated manifold, both during his lifetime and posthumously. This fact has been well summed up by Tucker Brooke writing on the English Renaissance in *A Literary History of England* (edited by Albert C. Baugh and published by Appleton-Century-Crofts, Inc., New York and London, 1948): "Nothing in Elizabethan literature, perhaps nothing until Byron's time, equaled the over-night fame of *Faerie Queene.* Spenser became at once 'the only living Homer' and the supreme literary celebrity of the age. Many other experts on Elizabethan literature will attest to the poetic supremacy of Spenser. The first collected edition of Spenser's works appeared in 1609; this was the first folio. The second folio appeared in 1611-1612-1613. The title-page of this last edition refers to him as "England's Arch-poët" as follows: "The Faerie Queen: The Shepheards Calendar, together with the other works of England's Arch-poët, Edm. Spenser. Collected into one volume, and carefully corrected. H. L. for Mathew Lowens, London, 1611-1612-1613."

"Actually the truth of the structure of *The Faerie Queene,* as well as of its meaning, lies undoubtedly somewhere between Graham Hough's dream-poem with concomitant dream-symbolism, Alastair Fowler's numerological symbolism, and William Nelson's intellectual and thematic solution."

Spenser's great fantasy is an Arthurian romance case in Virgilian epic-form. Like *The Aeneid,* it contains 12 books, or would have contained 12 books, if Spenser had lived to finish it; moreover, each book, like a smaller epic, is divided into 12 cantoes. Outwardly, it appears a discursive romance with acute allegorical features, or a unique type of allegory told in the form of a discursive romance.

The Faerie Queene is a dream-poem in the manner of the French medieval allegory *The Romaunt of the Rose,* by Guillaume de Lorris and Jean de Meung, which last inspired many similar works, and which was one of the first major works in literature deliberately to create an imaginary place as a background for a narrative. But whereas the *Romaunt* merely creates an imaginary garden, *The Faerie Queene* creates an entire land, an entire world, an entire cosmos, of the imagination, and one which somehow reflects the world we know. This is in itself a great feat of creative originality with Spenser. Also, whereas the *Romaunt* concerns itself mainly with love courtly and otherwise, the scope of Spenser's epic-poem is enormous: it attempts to reflect all of life, and not just human life.

The main or central structural principle of this enormous quasi-medieval dream-poem is most likely, as William Nelson contends, intellectual and thematic, that is, the central structural element is theme expressed through fable, allegory, and symbol. The centre or the central core is the principal theme of glory, or spiritual splendor, and gravitating around this arch-centre are the subsidiary centres or themes; but with everything guided or directed, in terms of over-all architectonics, by formal symbolic and/or numerological principles, as elucidated by Alastair Fowler: hence, a cosmic model, or a microcosmos reflecting the macrocosmos: if nothing else, the over-all cyclic movement of *The Faerie Queene* would indicate that the poem is a cosmic model. The result is Graham Hough's "Freudian" dream-poem: a high-fantastical Renaissance tapestry, replete with dream-symbolism as more or less understood in terms of *The Interpretation of Dreams* by Sigmund Freud (1900). And this brings us back, strangely enough, to the medieval dream-poem based ultimately on the fantastic allegory *The Romaunt of the Rose.*

Spenser undoubtedly derived the idea of the cyclic structure—as well as of the cyclic movement—of his epic-poem from the Arthurian and Carolingian mytho-poetic cycles. Further, the effect obtained by the typical Spenserian stanza is all part of the cyclic/circular ambiance created by Spenser for *The Faerie Queene*: a deliberate, usually slow-paced music as of a planet moving in its processional-like orbit around the sun; a music that purposes to reflect the order and harmony of the cosmos, or (more aptly) the music of the spheres; in the same way that the great circular maze which is the over-all structure of *The Faerie Queene,* purposes to reflect the great circular maze of the macrocosmos, of the stars and planets moving in their predestined orbits through the heavens.

It should be clear from the above that the present attempt at defining the over-all structure, movement, and

meaning of *The Faerie Queene* in no way excludes Émile Legouis's conception of Spenser's epic as a dream-like pageant of constantly evolving and dissolving imagery, and in no way excludes C. S. Lewis's conception of the poem as a grand pageant of the cosmos or of Nature and, hence, as Spencer's Hymn to Life. "A full interpretation of his [that is, Spenser's] genius, worthy of its theme," would cogently and harmoniously syncretize all these divers attitudes and approaches towards, as well as conceptions of, *The Faerie Queene.*

"Indeed, properly defined, *The Faerie Queene* not only presents the first conscious "olden" style in modern English,—or for that matter the first conscious style, or spectrum of styles, as we comprehend such tody,—but it also represents the first "Romanticism" (as understood in the sense of the Arthurian or Carolingian romances) as well as the first great "Gothic" fiction in modern English, in the most inclusive definitions of those expressions."

It may be argued that *The Shepheardes Calender* (1579) presents not only the first conscious "olden" and/or rustic style in modern English but simply the first conscious style, or spectrum of styles; except that we intend the statement above to be relevant to a conscious work of fiction, *qua* fiction, and not to a poeticized form of overt autobiography, which is what *The Shepheardes Calender* is in all verity. To the Elizabethans *The Shepheardes Calender* would have appeared more a *Portrait of the Artist as a Pastoral Poet* than anything else. This is not to deny the pivotal artistic

and historical significance of this earlier major poem by Spenser.

"For since around 1900, more or
less coinciding with the death of
Queen Victoria and with the inevitable
decline of the British Empire, *The
Faerie Queen* has fallen from the common currency that it once enjoyed in
the homes of English-speaking families
all over the world."

This statement, however extreme it
might appear at first, is perfectly true
in regard to the homes of the more
self-conciously   *cultured*   English-
speaking   families,   whether   they
formed part of the British Empire or
of the United States of America.

"If music and sweet poetry agree"

This sonnet is also attributed to
Richard Barnfield, but the present annotator agrees with Ernest de Selincourt that it seems much too good to
have as its author anyone other than
Shakespeare.

Avalonessys.

This is one of the comparatively few
original poems in verse included by
Michel de Labretagne in *La Jouvence
Bretagnesque,* and typically shows the
influence of the medieval and Atlantean lyric poetry that Labretagne studied with such care in his youth.

The Crown and Trident Imperial.
Through the French of Michel de Labretagne.

By an Atlantean poet of the Post-
Cataclysmic Age. The three principal
types of tridented crowns in ordinary
use throughout the Empire of Atlantis,
whether as heraldic silhouette or as
heraldry in the round, are as follows:

First, the archetypal crown and trident,
used simply to indicate Atlantis in
general, or by any royalty and/or any
kingdom in the Empire. Second, the
archroyal crown and trident, used exclusively by the Archroyal Family
and/or the Archkingdom. Third, the
thrice-tripled trident above the single
crown, the exclusive property of the
Archking, and handled only by himself
or any of his personal trident-bearers.

Atlantis.
Through the French of Michel de Labretagne.

The original sonnet, or song archroyal, Athallarion (ATH-uh-LARR-
ee-un) created about 13,000 B.C.,
shortly after the Great Cataclysm, the
which in a single day and night had
caused the submergence of virtually all
the Empire of Atlantis, including between one-third and one-half of Atlantis the Archkingdom, and including
Atlantis the great capital city of both
the Empire and the Archkingdom.
Athallarion was 97 at the time and
died soon after creating this his final
poem.

In recognition of his services to the
crown and state of Atlantis, and above
all for his great epic *The Song of the
Archking* (created for the 3,003rd-
Year Jubilee of the Empire of Atlantis), the last Archking, Atlas CLIII,
called Sfamoönophamos (SFAH-mo-
on-NOF-uh-moss; "born during the
epiphany of Sfamoön"), made him a
Grand Archknight Prince, and gave
him a series of vast estates in the
Great Vale to-West located in Poseidonis. In addition to his original title
of "Poet Laureate of Poets Laureate at
the Court of the Archking," Athallar-

ion assumed, at the behest of the Arch-king, the new title of "Prince of Poets and of Poets Laureate in All the Empire of Atlantis" especially created for him.

After the Great Cataclysm, this last great Atlantean poet journeyed from his estates in the Great Vale to-West in Poseidonis to the Outhanox (OO-thuh-nox), the Great Citadel of Poseidonis, to the south of which he now saw, instead of "The Sea of Verdure" that had been the Great Vale of Atlantis, the dark and turbulent waters of the Ocean Sea. It was this view, as well as the attendant extra-ordinary sense of loss common to all surviving Atlanteans, which inspired Athallarion's famous threnody.

Rose Escarlate.

Escarlate, thus in the original French title: the old French form for "scarlet"—from which derive both the English word and the modern French "écarlate."

"O Ebon-Colored Rose."
Through the French of Michel de Labretagne.

Created sometime before the 3,003rd-Year Jubilee of the Empire of Atlantis.

Your Mouth of Pomegranate.
Through the French of Michel de Labretagne.

Created by Prince Atlantarion during the wedding voyage of the Princess Aïs and himself amid the divers island kingdoms of the Empire of Atlantis; and in particular while visiting the is-land kingdom of Atkantharia (the Canary Islands), far-famed for her endless pomegranate-forests and for her ineffable wine of pomegranates.

The pronunciation of the word "pomegranate" used in this poem (as well as in number V of Sonnets on an Empire of Many Waters) is "POMM-uh-GRANN-it."

When We Were Prince and Princess.
Through the French of Michel de Labretagne.

Created by King Atlantarion and presented to the Queen Aïs on the occasion of their 30th wedding anniversary, and in memory of their wedding voyage amid the divers island kingdoms of the Empire of Atlantis, in the years just before the Great Cataclysm, when they were prince and princess. . . .

The Crown and Trident.
Through the French of Michel de Labretagne.

Created by King Atlantarion in the latter decades of his life, evidently sometime after the death of his belovèd wife, the Queen Aïs, but sometime just before the withdrawal of the Atlantean garrisons in what are now Ireland, Wales, and Cornwall.

The "crown and trident" was also both the principal coin of the realm and the basic medium of monetary exchange throughout the Empire of Atlantis.

Song.
Through the French of Michel de Labretagne.

From Athallarion's first collection *The Book of Athallarion,* the product of his first poetic youth.

"Thy Spirit Walks the Sea."
Dedicated to Nora May French, in memoriam.

Although born in Aurora, New York, 1881, Nora May French lived most of her 26 years in California, first in the Los Angeles area and then in San Francisco and Carmel just before she died. "Phyllis," a name she adopted while residing in the Los Angeles area, she preferred to "Nora May." She committed suicide—for her own good reasons, we may be sure—in November 1907 while a guest at the home of George and Carrie Sterling in Carmel. Her sister Helen (the present Mrs. Helen French Hunt) and a group of friends (the early group of Carmel writers and artists headed by George Sterling) with appropriate ceremony scattered her ashes into the Pacific Ocean from Point Lobos.

Henry Anderson Lafler, with the assistance of Sterling and the critic Porter Garnett, gathered and edited her verses which appeared posthumously in 1910, published simply as *Poems* by The Strange Company, San Francisco. The lines quoted to head the present tribute form the third and last stanza of the last poem included in her volume. Both Sterling and his protégé Clark Ashton Smith considered her one of the most naturally gifted poets of her sex ever to have appeared in America. She ranks as the West Coast equivalent of Edna St. Vincent Millay.

". . . This Lesbian promontory" (id est, "this promontory as of the isle of Lesbos") in line 1 of Mr. Fryer's poem is a deliberate reminiscence of stanza II of Swinburne's great elegy to Baudelaire, the *Ave Atque Vale*:

"For always thee the fervid languid glories / Allured of heavier suns in mightier skies; / Thine ears knew all the wandering watery sighs / Where the sea sobs round Lesbian promontories, / The barren kiss of piteous wave to wave / That knows not where is that Leucadian grave / Which hides too deep the supreme head of song. / Ah, salt and sterile as her kisses were, / The wild sea winds her and the green gulfs bear / Hither and thither, and vex and work her wrong, / Blind gods that cannot spare."

Sterling created two beautiful tributes to her, the sonnet *Nora May French* which begins "I saw the shaken stars of midnight stir" (collected in the volume *A Wine of Wizardry* etc., 1909), and the longer poem *The Ashes in the Sea / N. M. F.* (collected in the volume *The House of Orchids* etc., 1911). Clark Ashton Smith created a magnificent elegy in blank verse entitled *To Nora May French.* The title of the present tribute is a quotation taken from lines 76-77 of Smith's elegy: "But I will dream they spirit walks the sea, / Unpacified with Lethe." This elegy first appeared in Smith's collection *Ebony and Crystal, Poems in Verse and Prose,* published by the author himself in December 1922 at Auburn, California.

Recompense.
Through the French of Michel de Labretagne.

By an Atlantean poet of the Post-Cataclysmic Age.

To Edmund Spenser.

When Spenser's grave in Westminster Abbey was opened in the present century—not to recover the elegies to his memory which noblemen and poets had written and thrown into his grave at the time of interment; but to discover proof that Sir Francis Bacon had written the plays of William Shakespeare—neither poems, pens, nor remains were found; nor the proof the zealous pedants were hoping to discover. Since no remains were found, the truth can only be that Spenser was "translated" to the Court of Faeryland, indubitably at the express behest of his belovèd Faerie Queene.

Line 12: "You have completed your great song. . . ." Although *The Faerie Queene* as presently extant may be experienced as a complete work by the reader, formally it is unfinished. However, Spenser had every intention of completing it and, if his lifetime had proven equal to the task, had also every intention of creating a sequel of similar length to it, an epic revolving around King Arthur and His Knights of the Round Table, and most likely under such a title as *The Briton King*.

Line 14: "Both knight and poet laureate. . . ." Although Elizabeth I never knighted him—as odd as it might seem—Spenser did fill the position of poet laureate for the years 1590-1599.

Rose Verdastre.
Through the French of Michel de Labretagne.

Verdastre, thus in the original French title: the old French form for "greenish"—from which derives the modern "verdâtre."

Like the "little song" which begins "O ebon-colored rose," the product of

Athallarion's first poetic youth, and included in his first collection *The Book of Athallarion.*

A Fragment
Through the French of Michel de Labretagne.

By an Atlantean poet of the Post-Cataclysmic Age.

Lullaby.
Through the French of Michel de Labretagne.

Created for their children by Prince Atlantarion during the wedding voyage of the Princess Aïs and himself amid the divers island kingdoms of the Empire of Atlantis; and in particular while visiting the island kingdom of Atatemthessys (the Bermuda Islands), during their sojourn on the western end of the island.

Minor Chronicles of Atlantis.
Through the French of Michel de Labretagne.

General note: According to Labretagne, all of Prince Atlantarion's original "minor chronicles" were not poems in verse but were "purple patches" instead—that is, poems in prose.

Proem.

Pronunciations, etc. Aon: AY-on. Aïs: eye-EESS. Anorthys: uh-NORR-thiss. Ylliphya: ILL, lih-FEE-yuh or ill-LIF-fee-yuh (the northern shores of Africa, from Egypt to the western end of the Atlas Mountains abutting upon the Atlantic Ocean). Iffrikonn: IFF-rih-konn (Africa). Amphus: AM-fuss.

The Hippokamp.

Pronunciations. zaör: ZAY, ORE. hippokamp: HIH-po-kamp. hippokampos: HIH-po-KAM-poss. Aÿsius: eye-EE-see-uss. Poseidon: PO-see-DONN. taurokamp: TORR-o-kamp. leokamp: LEE-o-kamp. taurokampos & leokampos: in the same way as hippokampos.

The real sea-horse that still existed in the last days of the Empire of Atlantis, the French sculptor Marcel Loyau has magnificently reconstructed for the Clarence Buckingham Memorial Fountain located in Grant Park, Chicago, Illinois, immediately west of Lake Michigan. For this fountain (dedicated 26 August 1927) Monsieur Loyau conceived and executed four pairs of hippokampoi, situating each pair in each of the four corners of the fountain's great basin.

The Atlanteans also featured other creatures or devices, heraldic and otherwise, as figureheads on their ships and barges. The great central island, the Archkingdom, usually featured on her ships the mythical sea-horse; on the ships of her nobility and royalty a unicorned sea-horse who sported a crown or coronet around his neck and who brandished a trident at the end of his unicorn. Gades would feature on her ships a taurokampos or taurokamp. Atlantigades would feature a sea-satyr wreathed and crowned with grapes and grape-leaves. Atkantharia, a giant sea-scorpion. Iffrikonn-Yssthia, a leokampos or leokamp. Atalantessys, any one of several, characteristically gigantic flowers grown uniquely on that island. Atlantillia, a jaguär. Atatemthessys, a giant squid. At-Thulonn, a unicorned sea-horse, usually ermine-white. Aval-

onessys, a swan. Poseidonis, the mountain-heart-land of the Archkingdom, featured on her great barges (which floated adown the Amphus to the great imperial seat Atlantis) the giant sea-ram, half sea-monster, half wild-mountain-sheep. But almost always, above each of the huge eyes carven and painted on the prow (of every ship) high above the water-line, there would appear in bas-relief an archetypal heraldic sea-horse.

The River Called Amphus.

Pronunciations. Mythnom: MITH, nomm. Poseidonis: PO-see-DONN-iss. Monamphus: mo-NAM-fuss. At-Tho-Then: with an equal accent on each particle of speech. Poämphus: po-AM-fuss. Zaära: zay-ARR-uh. Zhaärth: zhay-ARTH. Outhanox: OO-thuh-nox. Xonorr: k'zo-NORR. Eiphlox: EYE-flox. Yllthyrrya: ill-THEER-e-uh. Izzarth: iz-ZARTH. Sfarnyx: SFAR-nix. Ampheum: am-FEE-um.

The Amphus Delta.

Pronunciations: Alphis: AL-fiss. Aälphis: ay-AL-fiss. Amnaältis: AM-nay-AL-tiss. Amphorial: am-FORR-ee-uhl. Amphamar: AM-fuh-MARR. Ataämphus: AT-uh-AM-fuss. Alphessys: al-FESS-iss.

The Imperial Crown Jewels of Atlantis.

Pronunciations. Murexidia: MYU-rek-ZIDD-ee-uh. Lemuria: lee-MYURR-ee-uh. Yndessys: in-DESS-iss. Yndessessian: IN-deh-SESS-ee-un. Mu: MOO.

"O high-spiring crown soaring over fifteen-hundred imperial feet into the air. . . ." An "imperial foot" was the basic metric unit in the Empire of Atlantis, and was established by Poseidon III from his own right foot as the ultimate authority over competing pedal measurements.

The Garden of Jealous Roses.

Pronunciations. Ataquor: AT-uhkworr. Lillittiss: LIH-lih-tiss.

The Tale of an Olden Love.

Pronunciations. Noöm: NO, omm. Naörthris: NAY, or-THRISS. Lailis: LEYE-liss. Ampara: am-PARR-uh. Aliddium: uh-LIDD-ee-um. Antillia: an-TILL-ee-uh. Ddath: DAHTH.

"Ampara, overwhelmed with grief and carrying his bardic lute, wandered forth from Noöm, never to return. . . ."

Virtually all Atlanteans, especially the young people, were singers and either musicians or poets, or both. Just as the purely musicianly lute (usually strung with eleven strings or more, and designed to be fretted by the fingers of the left-hand, and played largely by the fingertips of the right-hand) was a far more complex instrument than the purely bardic lute (usually strung with six strings, and designed—in the manner of the purely musicianly lute—to be fretted by the fingers of the left-hand, but played by the fingernails of the right-hand), similarly the bardic lute was far more complex than the bardic lyre but with one major difference from the purely musicianly lute: the bardic lute was employed less to create music per se than it was to create an appropriate ambiance for and around the poetry, and to space out the words, phrases,

and lines with a para-musical punctuation, but of such a simplicity that the poet could chord and pluck without distracting either himself or his audience from the poetry. Nevertheless, this ancient Atlantean, bardic-type accompaniment had predictably evolved into a highly complex art before the Great Cataclysm, and both the Prince Atlantarion and the last great Atlantean poet, to wit, Athallarion, were among the outstanding bardic-musical performers of their time. The zaör, or Atlantean harp and lyre combined, possessed certain distinct differences from the lute, being indeed closer to the basic seven-string lyre than to any other stringed instrument.

The Shepherd and the Shepherdess.

Pronunciations. Lailliquis: LEYElih-kwiss. Xilvaä: k'zil-VAY-uh. Lissarion: lih-SARR-ee-un. Atlantaon: AT-lan-TAY-on. Quolyx: KWO-lix. Septemmis: SEP-teh-miss.

Reciprocity.

Pronunciations. Pharanos: FARR-uhnoss. Ullfanon: ULL-fuh-nonn. Quomequa: kwo-ME-kwuh. Atlaïs Atalantossa: AT-leye-EESS AT-uh-lan-TOSS-uh.

Atalantossa, a name assumed by Atlaïs at her coronation, is that of the great Atlantean earth-mother-goddess within whom was essenced the Atlantean continent and about whom there centred elaborate cults throughout the Empire of Atlantis, especially in the kingdom of Gades.

The Iffinnix.

The Atlantean phoenix or iffinnix: IFF-in-nix.

Kilcolman Castle: 20 August 1965.
In the fellow-ship of Kirby McCauley.

Here, from about 1587 until October 1598, resided Edmund Spenser, the first great Elizabethan poet,—and by that token the first great English poet after Geoffrey Chaucer, as well as the first great poet in modern English,— and one of the greatest poets in English or any language. Here at Kilcolman Castle in County Cork, Ireland, Spenser created most of his mature poetry, including most of *The Faerie Queene.*

To this place, Mr. Fryer's great and good friend Kirby McCauley, of Minneapolis, Minnesota, then travelling in Ireland on vacation, made a pilgrimage on 20 August 1965, to pay homage to the elder bard, on behalf of the author at that time unable to make the pilgrimage himself. Subsequently, in his cards and letters to the poet for August, September, and October 1965, Kirby detailed his adventure at Kilcolman Castle, an adventure summarized in lines 1-9; hence, the Spenserian stanza was made possible only through the unique fellow-ship afforded by this friend. The castle, today scarcely more than an ivy-covered tower, is presently located on a private farm. No monument of any type whatsoever indicates that one of the greatest poets in English lived here for a considerable part of his life and created some of his greatest poetry here.

Aubade.
Through the French of Michel de Labretagne.

An early morning serenade created for their children by Prince Atlantar-

ion during the wedding voyage of the Princess Aïs and himself amid the divers island kingdoms of the Empire of Atlantis; and in particular while visiting the island kingdom of Avalonessys (in the Irish Sea), during their sojourn at Apenderragon the Great Watchtower in southern Valoth, or Wales.

The Lilac Hedge at Cassell Prairie.
Dedicated to August Derleth, in gratitude.

Cassell Prairie, Wisconsin, was founded by an English colony in the 1850's. "Cassell" is very probably an English place-name carried over to America, and is most likely not the name of one of the early settlers. The lilac hedge, more than half a mile in length, was planted by Deacon Cassell probably sometime in the 1880's, and is laid out in a straight line beside the road, with only three or four small breaks in it now. Not far from Cassell Prairie stands Place of Hawks, alias Arkham House, the home of August Derleth, which is located on the outskirts of Sauk City, some thirty miles northwest of Madison, the state capital. (Historical data courtesy of August Derleth.)

To Arkham House the author came on 25 May 1967 and stayed through the 29th. This was the author's first personal visit with Derleth at the latter's home even though their friendship had begun through correspondence in 1954. On three successive evenings (the 25th through the 27th) Derleth, Dennis Mack (one of Derleth's helpers), and the author visited Cassell Prairie while out on a drive in Derleth's car. The poem commemo-

dragoras, nenupahrs, etc.—all truly of monstrous dimensions—usually grouped in three's, with the central bloom higher than the two attendant ones).

The sixth of the ten island kingdoms, and the second of the third pair of the same, was different from the rest of the Empire in a number of unique ways. The chief island Atalantessys, just north of the equator, survives (in reduced form) as the St. Peter and St. Paul Rocks; about 400 miles to the southwest lay the two lesser islands Manthos (MAN-thoss) and Xalporal (zal-PORR-'l), which have survived (similarly in reduced form) as Rocas and as Fernando de Noronha Island, respectively. Manthos, which produced most of this realm's basic diet, lay about 200 miles northeast of the present-day Cabo de São Roque (that northeastern corner of the "nipple" on the great eastern-projecting "breast" formed by the subcontinent of Brazil); about 100 miles to the east (of Manthos) there lay Xalporal—the sixth greatest port in the Empire—whose entire coast, with multiple harbors large and small, served as the port of Atalantessys, and handled virtually all the trade and commerce coming from all along the entire eastern coast of what is today South America, from southernmost Lesser Antillia to the southernmost tip of the continent. Today the St. Peter and St. Paul Rocks, Fernando de Noronha, and Rocas are all Brazilian possessions.

About as large as Manthos and Xalporal combined, Atalantessys—an oval island wider east and west than north and south—served as the administrative and esthetic centre of the realm. The entire island, with her gently rolling terrain (low hills near the coast, and

slightly higher hills toward the centre), and with her eternal warm summer, resembled a great lush-green garden-park studded everywhere with palaces great and small. The principal residences of the kings of Atalantessys were two: the half-ruined Old Palace that spread all along the northern coast; and just inland of it, to the south, the New Palace, environed with elaborate formal gardens.

Although typically Manthos and Xalporal were tropically hot and wet, Atalantessys had an unexpectedly cooler climate than the jungle kingdom (that lay north-northeast of this southernmost realm of the Empire), due principally to the cold currents that came flowing out of the great southern ocean, bypassing Manthos and Xalporal to the west, and washing around this northernmost portion of the equator kingdom, or the garden kingdom (as it was also called on occasion). Accordantly the island lay at the centre of a vast and near-eternal cloud of fog and/or mist, which dissipated only on a few rare days during the entire year; at such times the heat and the light would prove almost unbearable; much of the vegetation that flourished in the cooler climate would wilt, some of it would die, and almost the entire population, human and otherwise, would seek the cooling waters along the coast or in the island's innumerable pools, lakes, and streams. It rained on Atalantessys virtually every day, once in the morning, once in the afternoon, and sometimes during the night; the rain fell heavier of course during the rainy season per se.

Due to the peculiar climate possessed by the chief island of the realm, as well as due to certain recondite fea-

tures of the soil, the Atlanteans cultivated uniquely on Atalantessys divers
gigantic flowers (many of them hy-
brids), much desired throughout the
Empire, and exported everywhere as
potted plants. These floral prodigies,
although most of them could not re-
produce, enjoyed nonetheless a long
life.

Carried on the cold currents coming
ultimately from the great frozen continent that lay far to the south, great
icebergs, in the ultimate season of
their dis-solution, would sail up offshore from out of the southern ocean.
The inhabitants of Atalantessys would
approach these ice-islands in their unireme barges, and then land thereupon,
to picnic and/or to explore the fantastic grottoes and other extra-ordinary
features of the icebergs' mutable architecture. Few or none were those who
mourned the passing or melting of
these icebergs as they constituted an
eternal menace to the shipping both of
the equator kingdom and of the Empire.

Atalantessys was about the same size
as Avalonessys—both were among the
smallest royal islands in the Empire—
and with his characteristic irony Poseidon III endowed this isle with the
name "Atalantessys" or "island kingdom of great Atlantis" when he sub-
sumed the realm into the Empire.

Sonnet VIII. *Atlantillia.*

Capital and principal port: Atzatlan
(AT-zuh-TLAHN).

Principal heraldic beast: the jaguär.

The so-called Pearl of the Antillias,
the rounded isle of Atlantillia lay between Greater Antillia and Lesser An-

tillia. But the island herself constituted
only a fraction of the total Atlantean
holdings in the twin Antillias; the seventh of the ten island kingdoms, and
the first of the fourth pair of the same,
included: the actual isle of Atlantillia
herself, the easternmost end of Greater
Antillia, and the northernmost end of
Lesser Antillia.

The land-mass of Greater Antillia
(on an axis running east and west, or
east and west-northwest) included the
present-day Cuba, Hispaniola, Jamaica,
Puerto Rico, and the Virgin Islands;
the eastern end of this near-continent
would be marked today at the southeast corner by St. Croix and at the
northeast corner by Anegada (more or
less due north of St. Croix). Lesser
Antillia (on a largely north-south
axis) included both the present-day
Leeward Islands and the Windward Islands; the northern or northwestern
end of this land-mass would be
marked today at the southwest corner
by Saba and at the northwest corner by
Anguilla (more or less due north of
Saba). Between what is now St. Croix
and Saba there stretched a low, narrow
isthmus—the Isthmus of Atzatlan or
Quoätzl (kwo-AT-z'l)—through which
the Atlanteans had excavated nine canals (which thus ran north and
south).

The last 100 miles or so of the
eastern end of Greater Antillia constituted Outer Atlantillia West, known
as the Itzl (IT-z'l), and the last 100
miles or so of the northern or northwestern end of Lesser Antillia constituted Outer Atlantillia East, known as
the Oöxochl (O-okk-ZO-k'l). Greater
Antillia and Lesser Antillia, centuries
before the arrival of the Atlanteans,

had formed a great unified empire, both politically and economically; the Antillian suzerain maintained his imperial seat in Quoätzl, a great city that once covered almost all of the island later named Atlantillia. When the Atlanteans settled here during the reign of Poseidon III, the great Antillian empire had long since disintegrated into divers rival territories, the island abounded with jaguärs, and the semi-tropical jungle had grown up over the ruins of the old abandoned Antillian capital Quoätzl.

The Atlanteans decided to maintain the island's plateau for the most part as a wild area, as a natural garden-park, and to build their city Atzatlan along the western, southern, and eastern shores of the island (this constituted Inner Atzatlan), as well as (just across the channel of Atzatlan Harbor) on the Isthmus of Quoätzl, along the easternmost shore of Greater Antillia, and along the northwesternmost shore of Lesser Antillia (all of these last three areas constituted Outer Atzatlan). Great gardened bridges joined the inner city to the outer. The Atlantillian kings built their palace in the northern part of the island's plateau and thus facing north out over the ocean.

Most of Atlantillia proper was covered by a plateau of moderate height with gently rolling terrain, but the entire realm enjoyed a semi-tropical climate, and thus was neither as hot or as wet as the jungle kingdom. The island kingdom of the jaguär was famous for extensive citrus forests (producing fruits which were similar to the present-day citron, lemon, orange, lime, grapefruit, etc.) located for the most part on the Itzl and the Oöxochl. The Atlan-

teans also cultivated in these areas one of the sacred fruits from the ancient continent of Mu, a fruit much like the present-day pineapple. Although she exported most of her fruit, Atlantillia imported most of her own food from the twin Antillias.

Atzatlan, the third greatest port in the Empire, handled most of the trade and commerce coming from Greater Antillia, Lesser Antillia, and the lands of Oöxathan (O-okk-zuh-THAHN; Central America), and all the other lands bordering on the Seas of Antillia (the western sea is the present-day Gulf of Mexico, the eastern sea is the present-day Caribbean).

North of the palace of the Atlantillian kings and upon a great bluff that looked out over the sea, there stood a curious outdoor thronehall yclept the Great Jaguär Throne, which faced east-northeast toward Atlantis the City. Here the Atlantillian king held regular audience unless wind or rain or both together prevented such.

The mere presence of the Atlanteans for some 3,000 years had created a comparative peace and sense of order (or harmony) amongst the warring Antillian chieftains and petty kings. Out of gratitude and courtesy the native Antillian peoples acknowledged the Atlantillian king as their nominal suzerain. Thus Atzatlan served as a focus for the political, economic, and esthetic life of the twin Antillias.

Line 9: "that further strand" or shore, in this case, could be either Outer Atlantillia West (that is, the Itzl) or the entire land-mass of Greater Antillia.

What was once the island proper of Atlantillia now lies at the bottom of

Anegada Passage, the channel which separates the Virgin Islands from the Leeward Islands.

Sonnet IX. *Atatemthessys.*

Capital and principal port: Meirion (MEER-ee-un).

Principal heraldic beast: the giant squid.

A large rounded island, the eighth of the ten island kingdoms, and the second of the fourth pair of the same, lay about 1,000 miles almost directly north (just a little to the west) of Atlantillia proper. Atatemthessys was originally, sometime during the dim geological past, an active volcano surrounded by a circle of other active volcanoes. The central volcano became extinct but the "wide round [about 300 miles across] of volcanoes sub-marine" remained. Within this orbit of volcanic activity and consequently warmer waters there lived not only the giant squid, the *Architeuthis princeps,* but many species of sea-life, including the archaic armored squid, that were extinct anywhere else in the oceans of the Pre-Cataclysmic world.

The Issvess Mountains dominated the interior of the island; this was a low, verdure-clad range, shaped like a great fish-hook, on an axis running northeast to southwest, with the "hook" at the southwestern end curling northward. The island was famous for her forests of fruit-trees, the principal ones under cultivation being similar to the modern peach, plum, cherry, apricot, etc. The peaches and apricots were about as large as modern grapefruits; the plums and cherries were about as large as apples. From these the Atlanteans made preserves, glacéd

fruits, wines, liqueurs, etc. The island was also famous for her honey and honey-bees, which she exported together with her fruits and fruit-products. Atatemthessys produced most of her own food.

Apart from a comparatively brief winter (rainy, windy, cool at night but warm during the day), the island kingdom of the giant squid enjoyed an exquisite spring climate the rest of the year, with a consequently lush semitropical vegetation.

The capital and principal port, to wit, Meirion, spread along the middle southern coast, facing south toward the southern and principal break in the wide round of undersea volcanoes,— the Gates of Atatemthessys (marked by a pair of colossal pharoses carved from towering chaotic masses of rose-flushed lava-stone tapering upwards).

The state palace of the kings of Atatemthessys rose up at the centre of Meirion but the ordinary residential palace, the Temthorial (tem-THORR-ee-ul) with its incredibly elaborate roof, stood in the middle of a vast garden-park located between the eastern shore of the island and the eastern end of the Issvess Mountains. The Temthorial and its principal throne-hall alike faced east toward Atlantis the City.

Atatemthessys—or island kingdom of the giant squid, or *atatemth* (the common Atlantean word for squid is "temth")—also exported jet-black inks, dyes, and cosmetics produced from the black "ink" of squids. The Atlanteans regarded cephalopods, especially giant squids, as essences or symbols of omnipotence, omniscience, and good fortune.

Line 9: "the flood and ebb of semitropic seas" does not refer to the *lunar* tides but to the comparatively low swell of the *solar* tides. The moon during Atlantean times was a small planet called Sfamoön (sfah-MO-on), with a weak orbit of its own, vacillating between the greater gravitational pull of Earth and Mars; it approached the Earth every five and six years in regular alternance; until finally, yielding to the greater gravity of Earth (at a time when Mars was at its furthest point away from both Earth and Sfamoön, and when the small planet itself was at its closest point to our own world), it was "captured"—thereby triggering the Great Cataclysm that spelt the end not only of the Atlantean Empire but, in addition, of virtually the entire Atlantean world as well.

As a result of the Great Cataclysm the "wide round of volcanoes sub-marine" became dormant and lapsed back into the ocean-floor, thus more or less completely disappearing. The Issvess Mountains of Atathemthessys have survived as the Bermuda Islands.

Sonnet X. *At-Thulonn.*

Capital and principal port: Ymnoth (IM-noth).

Principal heraldic beast: the unicorned sea-horse, usually ermine-white, and usually with a coronet around his neck.

Shaped roughly like a large diamond whose two lower sides are longer than the two upper sides; this ninth of the ten island kingdoms, and the first of the fifth and last pair of the same, lay (somewhat south of the present Cape Farewell) just off southeastern Greenland, the ancient Mhu Thulan (MOO, thoo-LAN), then as now covered with an ever-during mass

of ice, and fabled to have formed the ultimate peninsula of the legendary continent called Hyperborea. Heavily forested with evergreens and with such deciduous trees as were sturdy enough to flourish in this far northern latitude, the winter kingdom possessed a rolling terrain with low hills, very rocky in places, especially along the island's coast.

A great bridge (protected at either end with great castellated fortresses) of stone and crystal of divers textures and colors (fitted cunningly together without cement, and allowing for the contraction and expansion caused by the extreme changes in temperature from summer to winter) connected the island's northern point to the forested southern marge of Mhu Thulan which stretched from somewhere east of Cape Farewell to somewhere west of the present-day seaport Julianehaab.

This southern margin, called the Lonnthulan (LON-thu-LAN), and protected at her northern boundaries from the worst of the winter weather by great natural barriers of stone (which now form part of the high cliffs of Cape Farewell presently fronting the ocean at this southeastern tip of Greenland), served as a buffer for At-Thulonn against the terrible hyperboreal cold breathing off the great sheet of ice during the winter.

The winters here were very long; those in the kingdom of the unicorned sea-horse were not as long or severe as those in Mhu Thulan, due to the warm currents (coming ultimately from tropical and semi-tropical seas) washing around the island. With but a brief spring, summer, and autumn, the winter kingdom was usually self-sufficient in producing her own food during the warm weather (there were many small farms located all over the island) but she had to import most of her food for the long hyperboreal winter.

Located just south of the island's eastern point and with a magnificent harbor (but completely ice-free only during the warm weather which lasted some 90 days), the capital Ymnoth was the fourth greatest port in the Empire, and handled virtually all the trade and commerce coming from the eastern Seas of Naörth (NAY, ORTH; these stretched between Greenland and Norway, and included all the islands located within those waters as well as in the waters north of that stretch of ocean, as well as all the lands contiguous thereunto). To Ymnoth the Northkings would bring within their vessels —their dragon-headed uniremes—all manner of merchandise (smoked meats, smoked fish, lumber from northern trees, pelts and furs, etc.) in exchange for Atlantean products.

The state palace of the kings of At-Thulonn was located in the capital but the ordinary residential palace stood in the midst of the great royal estate that completely filled the island's southern point.

The northern lights actually unfurled their multi-colored veils all year round but the most spectacular displays occurred in autumn and in spring.

The unicorn that lived in the forests of southern and western Mhu Thulan, was ermine-white in winter and a delicate shade of light gray during the warmer weather (as contrasted to the perenially fawn-colored unicorn that lived in parts of Scotland, England, Ireland, and Wales). The female unicorn looked rather like a doe but with a long, pointed, convoluting horn issuing from her forehead. The male unicorn looked identical, but with that additional and nether horn unique to the male (this nether horn was just half as long but thrice as thick).

Super-gentle and super-timid animals, the unicorns were protected by royal and archroyal law—it was forbidden to kill them—and were therefore rarely hunted by most of the adventurous young people. The unicorn could only be captured through blandishments, through overt demonstrations of affection, in short, through love and kindness; but then the youth and the maiden capturing it had to let it go; however, only after they had convined the male or female unicorn of their enduring love for it.

Both the upper and lower classes hunted both on the ice-cap and in the Lonnthulan, as well as on the western coast of Greenland, from somewhere south of present-day Godthaab to somewhere north of present-day Godhavn on Disko Island. A variety of animals were hunted—deer, bear, fox, etc.—but in his sonnet on this island kingdom Athallarion has naturally selected for mention a more typically exotic assemblage such as the seal, the musk ox, and the caribou.

Nothing survives of this island kingdom save for a few rock formations projecting up out of the sea south of Cape Farewell but once contiguous to the northern end of the great bridge of stone and crystal that connected At-Thulonn to Mhu Thulan.

Sonnet XI. *Avalonessys.*

Capital and principal port: Ysstralot (ISS-truh-lot).

Principal heraldic bird: the swan.

The tenth and last of the ten island

kingdoms, and the second of the fifth and last pair of the same, lay more or less in the middle of the Shoaling Sea West (Irish Sea), almost equally distant from the middle southern shore of Ivvrinaä (IVV-rih-NAY-uh; Ireland), and from the westernmost points of Valoth (vuh-LOTH; Wales) and Karanak (KAR-ruh-nahk; Cornwall). Ivvrinaä connected at the northeast with Ultimate Allbeyonn (Scotland), and Allbeyonn (ALL-be-yonn; England) connected at the southeast with Nys (NISS; Europe) by the land-bridge Ym-Rith (IM, RITH), which sealed off at her eastern end the Shoaling Sea East (English Channel). Avalonessys herself, with rolling hills and with apple-orchards of great extent, enjoyed a near semi-tropical climate like that of the Scilly Isles, with such mild winters that apple-blossoms bloomed, and crops of apples ripened, all year round.

Celebrated for her forests of apple-trees and of rose-trees, this kingdom of the swan, the rose, and the apple, exported apples, all manner of apple-wines and apple-cordials, preserved apples, etc., as well as all manner of rose-clippings and roses, which the Atlanteans particularly cultivated on this island. What with the perennially light-green leaves of the apple-forests, this almost perfectly round island was about the same size as Atalantessys, and verily did resemble "A sea-green pearl in a shoaling sea"—the shoaling sea in question being the Shoaling Sea West.

The capital Ysstralot was displayed, together with her palatial suburbs, along the southern shore of the island, southwest to east-southeast. The state palace of the kings of Avalonessys rose up at the centre of the capital but, as in other island kingdoms, the regular residence was located outside the principal port and/or capital; in this case, on a low but vast and multi-terraced hill north of a large lake north of Ysstralot, all in the midst of great formal gardens.

We must make mention here of the extra-ordinary color, together with certain other peculiar and striking characteristics, of the two Shoaling Seas, the surface of which was rarely ruffled by other than the most moderate of storms, usually during the wintry season. As their name implies, these were comparatively shallow bodies of water with numerous bars of sand, and with a consequent color and over-all appearance rather like those of the seas around the Bahamas. The principal colors were yellow-green, green, dark-green, and aquamarine. Since much of the ocean-floor around Avalonessys was largely composed of a white sand comparatively free of marine growths, the over-all effect was, to say the least, unusual. When Athallarion descants of ". . . The Shoaling Seas' green crystalline flow—" (line 10) he is not indulging in any poetic exaggeration.

The name of Avalonessys, possessing as it does a double suffix, means "the island kingdom, or royal isle, or island realm, of apples." The single for "apple" is "aval" (uh-VAHL); the plural is "avalon" (av-uh-LONN). ("Avalonessys" was pronounced either "av-uh-law-NESS-iss" or, more rarely, "av-uh-LONN-ess-iss.") The "ys" or "is" designates of course "island," and the "ess" preceding it designates "kingdom" or "royal." "Nys"—the name for Europe—is a contraction for "nay is," which simply means "no island" or a continent.

There was a great cult in Avalonessys centering around the swan. The many lakes, ponds, and streams within the island served as resting places for all manner of migrant birds, but especially for the swans. The more extravagant of their admirers would cast small necklaces of Yndessessian pearls around the necks of the swans as they would float hither and thither and yon upon the surface of the island's "water-troves."

The only other places in the world at that time besides Mhu Thulan where the unicorn lived (to the best of the information available to the present annotator for the nonce), were parts of Ultimate Allbeyonn, Allbeyonn, Valoth, and Ivvrinaä. This unicorn (as contrasted to the ermine-white or pearl-gray unicorn that inhabited the southern and western coasts of Mhu Thulan) was a rich golden-fawn in color, but was as timid and gentle a beast as his brother species living north of At-Thulonn.

Many of the Atlantean forts and watchtowers in Ivvrinaä, Valoth, and Karanak have survived in varying ruinous conditions. However, nothing survives from the isle of Avalonessys herself save the memory and the name.

Sonnet XII. *Poseidonis.*

Capital and principal inland port: Xonorr (k'zo-NORR).

Principal heraldic beast: the giant sea-ram (the bottom half like that of the heraldic sea-horse, the top half the same as the head, horns, neck, and upper torso, but sans the legs, of the giant wild-mountain-ram).

See both the prose-poem *The River Called Amphus* and the note to this.

An elongated oval running west-northwest and east-southeast, Posei-

donis the Archprincedom possessed the highest mountains in the Archkingdom and hence in the Empire: three tremendous ranges, western, central, and eastern, called the Eiphlox Mountains. Their topmost peaks now survive, respectively, as the three main groups of the Azores. Leading Atlantologists, including the author of these notes, estimate that they rose at least as high as the Himalayas. There were two principal valleys in Poseidonis: the Great Vale to-West and the Great Vale to-East; although comparatively narrow east and west, they were as extensive north and south as the Great Vale of Atlantis.

Line 5: The Atlantean phoenix, or iffinnix, a semi-mythical bird reputed to live high in the central Eiphlox Mountains. Hence, any eminence ascending "Beyond the heights whereto the phoenix flies," is indeed of an extra-ordinary height.

At the northern end of the Great Vale of Atlantis, where the western and the eastern branches of the Poämphus met in the great lake yclept the Gates of Day (wherefrom flowed the eastern branch of the Amphus River); and on the verge of the plateau lying thus at the southern base of the central Eiphlox Mountains; there stretched the Outhanox, the Great Citadel of Poseidonis, along an east-west axis. The Citadel served as a fortress to the city just north of it, to wit, Xonorr (this metropolis was one of "the Seven Cities" figuring in one of the Archking's official titles, to wit, "King of the Seven Cities"). Lying thus long and low (there was only one principal storey but arranged on two or three main levels), the Outhanox possessed a great battlemented southern terrace which ran along the southern verge of the plateau, crowning thus a series of great stone palisades, and looking out into the upper or northern reaches of the Great Vale of Atlantis, or "The Sea of Verdure" as it was called.

To the Outhanox there were brought, from all the ten kingdoms, the dead kings and queens who, after suitable mummification and enrobement, sat enthroned along both walls of the seemingly endless halls and corridors. At the time of the Great Cataclysm, the Outhanox ensepulchred over 150 generations of kings and queens from all over the Empire; thus, there were over 3,000 crowned heads.

When after the fall of Atlantis the City to the Northkings the child-king Poseidon II (PO-see-DONN), called the Son, fled north with his court and with such of the Atlanteans as had not been enslaved by the Northking invaders; it was here in Poseidonis that they set up their temporary government in exile as it were, a kingdom that was to endure through the three hundred years of the great feudal age that preceded the Empire of Atlantis. After winning back the Atlanteans' first realms in the south of Atlantis, after conquering the entire island, and then after establishing the Empire on an official basis; Poseidon III, called the Earth-Shaker, the Empire-Builder, the First Lord of Sea and Land, etc., made Atlantis the City—now recovered from the Northkings—the capital of his empery. But the old city in the north, the old Citadel, and the entire upland country, remained the spiritual home of the Atlanteans. They thus always cherished an especial affection for Poseidonis, a cradle-realm of empire and of mighty kings, and a place of refuge when the Atlanteans' very life and culture were threatened with extinction.

Officially the Archprincedom was virtually the equivalent of one of the ten island kingdoms. The Heir Apparent, usually the Archking's eldest son, the Archprince, maintained his court in the old Citadel. In his governing of the Archprincedom he would pass his apprentice-kingship. Thus, when upon the incapacity or retirement or death of the old Archking, the Archprince came to the supreme throne of the Empire, he had usually proven himself a thoroughly experienced ruler.

One of the five principal divisions of the Archkingdom, Poseidonis grew a variety of crops in abundant harvest, and together with the Vale of Mythnom, as well as the island kingdom of At-Thulonn,—and together with the great northern prong of Atlantis, as well as all the high mountain-lands of the Archkingdom,—the Archprincedom enjoyed a true cycle of the four seasons. The name of the Archprincedom, styled thus after Poseidon II (as well as in memory of Poseidon I, called the Father), simply means "island of Poseidon"—the island in question referring to the great "island of mountains" which was Poseidonis rising up from within the midst of the Archkingdom.

Sonnet XIII. *The Merchant-Princes.*

Line 14: "the arch Acropolis" (as in line 2 of the earlier sonnet *The Crown and Trident*): that is, the leading acropolis in all the Empire of Atlantis.

Once every thirty days the Archking would summon all the great merchants and merchant-princes resident in and around Atlantis the City, to meet him at dawn within the Place (or Plaza) Acropolitan, just outside the Great Gate Acropolitan which afforded unique access to the Acropolis from the Plaza and from the City. But, although he would summon them to meet him there at dawn, the Archking would sometimes make them wait upon his late arrival, and sometimes he would not appear at all; however, only after making them wait upon him a due period of time, thus merely to show them that there were indeed some power or authority higher than their own merchantry.

Sonnet XIV. *An Argosy of Trade.*

A word of explanation is needed here to detail certain distinct peculiarities about not only the Atlantean trireme but about the Atlantean galleys in general,—unireme, bireme, quinquireme, etc. Unlike the galleys used in the Middle Ages or in classicial antiquity—which were large, low, usually one-decked, usually flat-bottomed, and propelled by both sails and oars—the Atlantean oar-banked vessels were ocean-going ships which—while certainly large, and while propelled by both sails and oars—sat high in the water, were usually multi-decked (rather like a galleon, all proportions guarded), and always equipped with a deep, large, and permanent keel designed not only as part of the over-all engineering of a given vessel but principally for sailing over the deep waters of the Ocean Sea.

Sonnet XV. *Memories of the Astazhan.*

Created by Aänsess (AY-ahn-sess) in Valoth (vuh-LOTH) but a year or so before the Great Cataclysm, and in memory of his birthplace, the Astazhan (AH-stuh-ZHAHN).

The great prong of southeastern At-

lantis, and one of the five principal divisions of the Archkingdom, the Astazhan occupied a vast pastoral plateau surrounded by low coastal mountains on the west, south, east, and northeast, and by inland mountains of a largely medium height on the north and northwest (these last were the southernmost ranges of the eastern Eiphlox Mountains). This area enjoyed outstanding fame not only for its dairy products, especially for magnificent and variegated cheeses, but also for dairy cattle, which the local dairy merchants exported throughout the Empire, out through Atlantis the City and her merchant fleets, of course.

Many distinguished persons had been born in the Astazhan, including the last Queen Consort Archroyal, to wit, Atlaïs Quolaïtho (AT-lie-EESS KWO-lie-EE-tho). A woman of great beauty, charm, distinction, and intelligence, as well as a poetess of considerable originality and accomplishment, Quolaïtho bore Atlas CLIII, called Sfamoönophamos (SFAH-mo-on-NOF-uh-moss), seven daughters and nine sons. The last-born son was the youngest child of the Archking, to wit, the famous poet Prince Atlantarion whose marriage to the Princess Aïs of Ylliphya became one of the marvels of late Atlantean and Post-Cataclymic poetry and romance.

Aänsess was one of the last great masters of the song archroyal.

Sonnet XVI. *A Letter from Valoth.*

Created by Aänsess at Apenderragon (AH-pen-DARE-uh-gonn) the Great Watchtower in southern Valoth during the first three days following the Great Cataclysm, and dictated by him to his scribe on the third day.

In a single day and night, as veraciously described by Plato himself (in his principal accounts of the Atlantis Mythos, to wit, the dialogues yclept the *Timaeus* and the *Critias*), the Great Cataclysm—preceded and accompanied by a succession of terrific earthquakes and earthquake waves—had lowered extensive areas of the ocean-floor, and had caused the submergence of virtually all the Empire of Atlantis: all of the nine lesser island kingdoms, and between one-third and one-half of the Archkingdom. Of the nine lesser island kingdoms, nothing survived above the waves but a comparatively few mountain-peaks. Of the Archkingdom herself, there survived only the great mountain-ranges, including the central mountain-heartland Poseidonis. The great prong of southeastern Atlantis, the Astazhan, also survived.

Only the fact that they were visiting Poseidonis on official business just prior to the Great Cataclysm, and prior to their scheduled return to the capital of Atlantis, preserved the King Atlantarion and his own immediate family from the general destruction. They had gone to Xonorr, the capital of Poseidonis, in order to ensepulchre within the Outhanox the Pan-Atlantean royalty, most of whom had perished in the catastrophic Battle Before Athens but a short period of time before.

In his accompanying commentary in prose, Aänsess informs Atlantarion that the highest earthquake waves had washed the foot of the huge battlemented walls environing the Great Watchtower. Apenderragon, it must be noted, crowned an only slightly lower spur of one of the highest mountains in southern Wales, or Valoth, and commanded from this eminence a sweeping panoramic view of the Shoaling Sea West and of Avalonessys herself lying in the middest thereof.

The waves caused by the submergence of Avalonessys, and by the lowering of the ocean-floor of the Shoaling Seas both East and West—terrible as these waves may have proven—were nothing compared to those caused by the accompanying submergence of one-third or one-half of the Archkingdom. These last waves came rolling out of the west, the southwest, and the south, only a little later than the waves created by the sinking of Avalonessys.

While the geological causes and forces that created the Great Cataclysm had been building up for an extremely long time, it has now been established beyond any doubt that it was the "capture"—by and into Earth's orbit—of our later moon, the small planet Sfamoön (sfah-MO-on), which triggered the grand catastrophe—with its attendant outrageous earthquakes and earthquake waves—which not only submerged most of the Empire of Atlantis but swept away most of the Atlantean world as well.

Sfamoön, with a weak orbit of its own, had been vacillating for eons between the greater gravitational pull of Earth and Mars. It would approach the Earth every five and six years in regular alternance. It was at the end of these five-year and six-year periods that the Pan-Atlantean royalty, together with many other Atlanteans of all classes, would gather to Atlantis the City from all over the Empire: in order to reconsider the old laws, to codify new commandments (which would sometimes change or modify the old ones), to discuss common interests, to resolve any problems affecting any and all parts of the Empire, to plan the common future, and to hold high festival for thrice-thirty days, etc. This was the Grand Council of the Kings—the Atlantean festival of festivals—a kind of combination Easter-Thanksgiving-Christmas-and-New-Year.

By a supreme irony, the closer epiphany or manifestation of Sfamoön almost invariably happened at the time of the vernal equinox—which marked not only the Atlantean New Year but also the official commencement for the Grand Council of the Kings. Sfamoön was thus the particular star of good fortune to the Atlanteans, associated by them with their festival of festivals, and thus with all things joyously beginning anew. However, at the time of the last regular manifestation of Sfamoön, Mars was at its furthest point away from both Earth and Sfamoön, and the small planet itself was at the closest point it had ever been to our own world. Yielding finally to the superior gravity of Earth, Sfamoön was "captured"—yet its greater proximity was now to bring only death and destruction to the Atlantean world.

The actual Cataclysm occurred about a year after the "capture" of Sfamoön; during that one year our new satellite changed visually from a large star of dazzling brilliance into the familiar silver disk the size of a small coin that we now know. Also during that one year, the oceans of the world came increasingly to feel, in addition to the old and gentle *solar* tides, the new and increasingly greater *lunar* tides. Thus, following the Great Cataclysm, a succession of tremendous waves—unutterable in the havoc and the destruction they created—battered the shores of the entire basin of the North Atlantic Ocean, but the effects of these waves were manifest in all the oceans of the world, especially the Seas Within the Gates of Gades (the twin basins of the Mediterranean). The waters of the Ocean Sea burst through the great land-bridge at the Gates of Gades (which connected Gades to Iffrikonn), creating the present Straits of Gibraltar therethrough, and then burst through the great land-bridge between the present Sicily and Tunisia, creating a permanent passage therethrough, also. Thus, the two great basins of the Mediterranean were joined, and the over-all sea level was raised to its present measure. The tremendous waves caused by the Great Cataclysm gradually lessened everywhere over a period of many days. In consequence of the lowering of their ocean-floor, both Shoaling Seas had assumed the darker hues of other seas—now being indistinguishable therefrom—and had thus lost forever their former characteristic hue of green and aquamarine.

O Splendor sunk, alas! beyond recall,
*   that once of yore*
Her crown and trident's empire stretch-
*   ed from east to western shore. . . .*

Alas! And now no more . . . For ever
*   more. . . . Alas!*

* * *

Forevermore? Perhaps there shall rise
*   yet in far-off time,—*
Beyond this bleak, blind interim of
*   now and nevermore,—*
Many a new Atlantis from "the cosmic
*   sea sublime". . . .*

And there, perhaps, in future gardens
*   marvellous and vast,*
Shall bloom again all splendor and all
*   beauty lost and past.*

Two thousand copies of this book have been printed by The Collegiate Press, George Banta Company, Inc., Menasha, Wisconsin, from Linotype Garamond on Winnebago Eggshell. The binding cloth is Holliston Black Novelex.